Consumer Behavior

D1416777

Consumer Behavior

Women and Shopping

Patricia Huddleston

Michigan State University

Stella Minahan

Deakin University

FREE PUBLIC LIBRARY, SUMMIT, N.J.

Consumer Behavior: Women and Shopping
Copyright © Business Expert Press, LLC, 2011.
All rights reserved. No part of this publication may be reproduced,
stored in a retrieval system, or transmitted in any form or by any
means—electronic, mechanical, photocopy, recording, or any other
except for brief quotations, not to exceed 400 words, without the prior
permission of the publisher.

First published in 2011 by
Business Expert Press, LLC
222 East 46th Street, New York, NY 10017
www.businessexpertpress.com

ISBN-13: 978-1-60649-167-6 (paperback)

ISBN-13: 978-1-60649-168-3 (e-book)

10.4128/9781606491683

A publication in the Business Expert Press Consumer Behavior
collection

Collection ISSN: forthcoming (print)
Collection ISSN: forthcoming (electronic)

Cover design by Jonathan Pennell
Interior design by Scribe, Inc.

First edition: January 2011

10 9 8 7 6 5 4 3 2 1

Printed in Taiwan

3 9547 00358 7875

Abstract

What does shopping mean to American women? This question is the focus of our book. We profile the American woman and examine how life has changed since her grandmother was young. Women have many choices about when and where to shop; thus retailers need to understand her needs and wants to attract and maintain her business.

We provide a brief history of retailing in the United States to show how the retail industry has changed as women's lives have changed. Malls have contributed to the development of contemporary society, particularly as a site for relaxation and social connections outside of the home. We examine shopping as a life skill and a craft that is taught, both indirectly and deliberately by parents, particularly mothers.

Our research identified five distinct types of shoppers. Most women tended toward or were clearly identifiable as one of these five types. We delve into each shopping typology and discuss the underlying motivations for the shopping behavior in each group. We discuss identity and creativity, power and independence, seeking solitude, emotional release, and companionship as motivations for shopping and what these mean to the retailer.

Some women love and others loathe shopping. Our goal in this book is to alert retailers, merchandisers, property developers, and manufacturers about the major dos and don'ts to appeal to women. Retail is detail and it is easy to get the simple elements wrong, leading to unhappy customers. For example, we analyze what women want from retail sales staff and explore the customer and sales assistant relationship and its importance to women.

Will shopping remain a female activity or will a new gender balance develop? What are the two consumers segments that present huge opportunities to the retail industry? Insights to these questions are provided in the last chapter.

Key Words

women, shopping, consumer socialization, social shopping, experiential shopping, hedonic, utilitarian, shopping malls, mothers, and daughters

Contents

CHAPTER 1

An Introduction to Women and Shopping

Why a book on women and shopping? Why is it important? How do women shop and what does it mean to them? How can marketers and retailers maximize the appeal of their products to women? This book provides a wealth of background information and detailed insights into the topic of American women and shopping. The book is written specifically for business professionals in the following areas:

- marketing
- apparel and household goods manufacturing
- distribution and supply
- small to medium enterprise (SME) owners
- retailers
- advertisers
- property developers
- mall managers

So why write a book about women and shopping? Because of their consumer spending power, women are crucial to survival in the competitive retail industry in America. Women matter because, worldwide, they control so much of consumer spending. Women's earning power worldwide is expected to reach $18 trillion by 2014.[1] In addition to their earning power, women also have tremendous influence over total consumer spending. Currently, they control $20 trillion in spending, and by 2014 that figure will increase to $28 trillion.

Today's women are better educated, have more financial power and decision-making abilities, and have greater mobility than any previous generation of women. They are a formidable influence on the entire retail supply chain from source, to store, to consumption, and to disposal.

We acknowledge that men, particularly of Generation X and Generation Y, are becoming more comfortable with shopping and retailers are providing focused offerings to them, particularly in fashion, health, and beauty. Yet it is the female consumer who reigns supreme, often directly influencing the decision-making of the male shopper. Retailers, marketers, and suppliers who ignore or inadequately respond to the wishes of the female consumer do so at their own peril.

This book provides a fascinating insight into women's shopping habits and motivations. The book is of interest to business professionals as they will gain a better understanding of the most powerful economic force in the retail industry. Women in contemporary American society are able to shop in a way that their grandmothers would not have dreamed about. Far more than previous generations, women today have more power, are better educated, have far more resources, and are able to make their own decisions—they shop because they can!

"Tell me about you and shopping." When we posed that question, we were greeted with good humor and friendly banter. Then women begged us to listen to their favorite shopping stories, demonstrating the importance of shopping in their lives.

The book emerges from our interviews with women, aged 18 to 74, from all over America. They talked to us about how important shopping is in their lives and how dominant shopping is for them socially, extending to their leisure time and their holidays. Patricia Huddleston is a professor of retailing at Michigan State University, teaching students about the science of retail strategy. She has published widely in academic journals and regularly presents her research at conferences. Stella Minahan is a senior lecturer at Deakin Graduate Business School in Australia. She has studied the shopping habits of women in Australia, South Africa, and England. She has profiled several shopping styles and here reports on the shopping styles of American women. We follow women all across America on their shopping trips and share their favorite, funniest, and most poignant moments in the malls. After reading this book, you will have an understanding of the importance of women and shopping to the U.S. economy in general and to the retail industry in particular. You will understand that when women go shopping, they can have a great time even if they don't buy a thing. Shopping is more complex than making a purchase. We found recurring themes for shopping motivations include the need for power and independence, creativity and self-identity, and meeting emotional needs.

What motivates this behavior? How can retailers and marketers respond? The challenge for retailers and property developers is to create an environment so that women do the following:

- have a wonderful experience in the mall
- have a positive response to the brands
- make purchases
- make return visits

The insights in the chapters are for the retail industry generally, and we make suggestions for ways to increase market share by being more knowledgeable and responsive to customers.

This chapter continues with a definition of shopping as we start to explore why women shop. The next question posed is why women matter to the retail industry. In brief, women matter because they are key decision makers in consumer spending. Women are astute and experienced shoppers and must be treated accordingly. Women matter because of their power in consumer spending and because they are crucial to survival in the fiercely competitive retail industry in America. Retail is a crowded industry and only the best survive.

We also review what is known about the way that female biology and sociology affect the way women shop as compared to men. In this chapter, we also profile the contemporary American woman and conclude with an introduction to the remainder of the book. So, what is shopping?

So, What is Shopping?

Shopping, by definition, is "to examine goods or services with intent to buy; to hunt through a market in search of a best buy; and to make a search."[2] Shopping can be roughly divided into two main types or categories: convenience and recreational shopping. Researchers divide reasons for shopping into hedonic and utilitarian motivations. Hedonic shopping refers to shopping for pleasure and appeals to "the multisensory, fantasy, and emotive aspects of one's experience with products."[3] On the other hand, utilitarian shopping is motivated by shopping as a task, with product acquisition as the goal. We didn't set out to focus on either category; we let the women themselves guide that process. In general terms, the women we interviewed were more interested in discussing recreational (hedonic) shopping—that is, the shopping trips that can do the following:

- be leisurely
- involve some elements of fun
- solve problems
- include seeing new fashions and trends
- just be the experience of strolling

Shopping is certainly not just about buying something, as the women have so clearly said. Shopping is much more than opening the wallet and flashing the plastic. In fact, some shopping trips are made without a purchase, or at least not a planned purchase. Other trips might involve only buying a coffee. Shopping for women is certainly about buying but it is also about leisure, creativity, pleasure, and independence.

We did not ask our interviewees to define shopping. What happened in the majority of interviews is that when the women talked about shopping, they talked about clothes and accessories shopping for themselves. Very few women mentioned the run of the mill domestic grocery shopping. That seems to be an activity that is not considered "shopping." It is considered to be a routine activity that is undertaken differently. One of our interviewees said that she loves to clothes shop and to go for groceries but they are very different activities for her:

RESPONDENT: But I . . . I approach them very differently. Like grocery shopping is very systematic for me, I think about what I'm going to cook for the next week or so, make a list of what I'm going to buy and then go in and pretty systematically, up and down the aisle in the grocery store, purchase what I need to purchase. Don't usually get things that aren't on my list.
INTERVIEWER: So it is planned and structured.

RESPONDENT: It's very . . . it's very structured, yeah, it is. Which is totally different from any other kind of shopping.

Why Women Matter

Why do we need to consider women at all? There are arguments in the consumer behavior literature that lead to the focus on women and consumption in this book. In particular, the issue of gender is rarely a significant part of consumption research according to consumer behavior researchers.[4]

Why should the average retailer pay any attention to the opinions and needs of women? The reasons are as follows:

- decision-making and financial power
- the powers of loyalty and recommendation

The Decision-Making and Financial Power of Women

Women call the shots in the vast majority of consumer spending decisions. In America, women buy or influence 80% of consumer purchases. The group between 18 and 24 years of age alone possess $11 billion a year in disposable income.[5] Women decide what type of house is bought (91%) and how it will be furnished (94%). Women buy approximately 60% of all cars and influence the decision in approximately 90% of all car purchases. Women purchase over 51% of consumer electronics and 50% of computers (both traditionally male-driven markets).[6]

In contemporary society, women head many households and earn more than their partners in approximately 20% of cases. They may not earn the most money but they certainly have the decision-making power.[7] The female customer knows that she has that power and is not afraid to use it. Female consumers are powerful purchasers yet there are very few studies on how they shop.[8] Women have become the primary purchaser, yet are still overlooked.[9] There is so little research undertaken into women as consumers that it has been said that it is one of the major business knowledge gaps in recent decades.[10]

Most of the research into marketing and retail has focused its attention on a variety of segments in an effort to understand and reach the consumer. Why should we now turn our attention to women? The simple answer is because women make up over half of the population and are responsible for more than half of the spending.[11] In fact, many men would recognize the familiar view of there being "my money and our money" when it comes to how women divide the household finances.

American women are freer, better educated, healthier, and spend more time out of the house than at any other time in history. Their participation in the paid and unpaid workforce is increasing, both in full-time and part-time positions. They are remaining single longer, having children later if at all, and climbing the corporate ladder higher and faster.[12]

The female shopper is the most important force in the American economy. She influences what we eat, what we wear, what we read, the furniture we sit on, and the cars we drive, what we use to grind beans for coffee, squeeze fruit for juice, and all manner of items right down to the toilet paper in the bathroom. and the sheets we sleep on. For too long the retail industry has not understood why women shop. Management guru Tom Peters makes the following remarks:

> This women's thing is unmistakably in my opinion economic opportunity number one. Bottom line: Financial services companies don't get it. Hospitality companies don't get it; even two thirds of health care employees are women. God alone knows automobile companies, with a half trillion dollars in retail sales in the U.S alone, don't get it.[13]

Any retailer that "doesn't get it" is quite simply missing the greatest opportunity of all.

The Power of Loyalty and Recommendation

It is important to understand the financial and decision-making power of women. Another, perhaps even more important topic, is the power of their loyalty and their ability to make recommendations to their friends and colleagues. Shopping is women's business and they take their responsibilities seriously. The role of women is changing, but still women are the main shoppers. Women are able to help grow and support or to damage a retail business solely by word of mouth. They are superb communicators and will share their shopping experiences with their friends. Positive shopping experiences are recounted with pleasure and word gets around that a retail outlet is providing good value or a new exciting offer. More powerful is the spread of bad news. The word is spread far and wide about a poor shopping experience. An aggrieved female customer will tell many people of her disappointment. And she will tell the story for years to come. Shopping is still, and always will be, a predominantly female activity, and women are capable of causing an entire species of retailer or product to fail if they can't adapt to their needs.[14] Women are making their presence known in traditionally male purchasing areas such as autos, consumer electronics, and computers, yet in many cases they are not receiving the treatment they deserve. Some retailers, particularly in traditionally male-dominated environments like car repair shops and electronics stores, are still not providing women with the service that they need and deserve. The auto industry is changing slowly, but still women can feel patronized, scorned, and "ripped off" in these male-dominated environments.[15]

Generations of Loyalty

It is clear that there is a very strong connection between one generation of women and the next. Most mothers will take every opportunity to educate their daughter in the ways of shopping, including making recommendations or condemnations of particular retailers. Serve women well and you can have a loyal customer for a very long time, particularly if the next generation inherits that loyalty from their mothers. We heard of women who encouraged their children to buy from particular retailers that served their mothers well. In our mobile society and with the advent of national retail chains, store loyalties nurtured in childhood can also transcend community boundaries and follow women as they move.

American Women

The current population of women in the United States is just over 150 million, making it well nigh impossible to present a single profile of American women. In this section, we present and comment on the key attributes of education, employment, fertility, life expectancy, levels of poverty, and personal wealth as compared to men. Here the scene is set for the following chapters. This chapter answers the question, "Why care about women and shopping?" To answer these questions we look back and discuss how women's lives differ from the lives of their mothers and grandmothers. Women are now better educated, have more financial power and decision-making abilities (including control of their fertility), and greater mobility than previous generations. Yet these advances come with a range of stresses including little time for them to be and do whatever they want to do.

Education Attainment

The number of women going on to earn higher education credentials has increased dramatically over the last half century. Over 30% of women are high school graduates and nearly 20% of all American women hold a Bachelor's Degree; interestingly, men and women are equally as likely to be college graduates.

Women's Work

According to the U.S. Bureau of Labor Statistics, women hold 49% of available jobs in the United States. The combination of work and household duties puts a lot of pressure on working women. In most cases, women are still expected to maintain the household and remain responsible for domestic chores (including shopping). According to the American Time Use Survey (2008) on an average day, 50% of women and 20% of men did housework. Women spend an average of 3.5 hours per week shopping for consumer goods; men spend about 2 hours per week (75% less time than women). This shopping is utilitarian (e.g., food shopping), not the hedonic shopping experiences our interviewees spoke about enthusiastically.

Life Expectancy and the Baby Boomers

Life expectancy has improved significantly for both women and men in the last 50 years. According to the National Center for Health Statistics (2009),[16] on average, a female born in 2010 can expect to live for nearly 81 years and a male born in 2010 can expect to live for nearly 76 years.

Unfortunately, life expectancy for the African American population is still lower than the general population.

Personal Earnings

As of 2007, American women still earn substantially less than men, on average, 78 cents to every dollar that a man earns (see Table 1.1). Thus, while women control the lion's share of retail spending, that total is less than it could be. For example, with U.S. retail spending at 3.3 trillion dollars (2007), if women's earnings were on a par with men's, the potential spending power would increase 22% to 4.03 trillion dollars per year. Put another way, it would be like putting more than $13,000 in the hands of every U.S. citizen.

Sociological and Biological Differences in Shopping Behavior

Sociologists believe[17] that gender is more than a biological matter. A person's gender is not just a matter of DNA and chromosomes. It is also built by the culture surrounding the individual. Societies treat and raise men and women differently and the roles of men and women will vary according to the society they live in. A particular

Table 1.1. Mean Earnings by Highest Degree Earned, in U.S. Dollars: 2007

	Not a high school graduate	High school graduate	Some college No degree	Associate's degree
Female	15,315*	24,234	26,527	33,276
Male	24,985	36,839	39,375	47,190
	Bachelor's degree	Master's degree	Professional	Doctorate
Female	43,127	54,772	83,031	69,251
Male	70,989	86,966	142,282	108,941

* refers to constant 2007 dollars

Source: From U.S. Census Bureau (2007). Current population survey. Retrieved February 15, 2010 from http//www.census.gov/population/www/socdemo/educ-attn.html

society will have a set of expectations of behaviors, roles, stereotypes, and personality traits that will determine the masculine and feminine differences in that society.[18]

Throughout their lives, males and females are socialized into their gender roles as they receive cues on what is "normal." The signals come from parents, friends, teachers, history, and the media.[19] We learn about what is "normal" at an early age. The norms associated with being "masculine" or "feminine" are learned and adopted and play a large part in the development of our gender identity.

Some years ago, a study looked at the effect of cultural gender roles and stereotypes on Christmas gift shopping. It was found that Christmas shopping was considered "women's work" because of traditional gender roles. A person's gender also influences the type of socialization that people experience. That experience influences the kind of consumer activities they will be involved with. For example, women (more than men) would be socialized to view Christmas shopping as an important task through observing or assisting their mothers, and therefore would presumably be more involved in the activity.[20]

A person's gender explained significant differences in the following characteristics:

- the number of gifts bought
- the month shopping began
- hours spent shopping per gift
- reported success

We can conclude that although a person's biology plays a major part in how and what they do, the society in which a person is raised is highly influential as well. These cultural influences are present from birth and may have a significant role in explaining the gender differences in shopping behavior. They may also explain the socialization of women to view shopping as a predominantly feminine activity.

Consumer behavior in general, and shopping in particular, is one of many areas where the differences between men and women become clear.[21] Consumption is an activity with a gender-pervasive filter through which individuals experience their social world; "consumption activities are fundamentally gendered."[22] This perception of gender leads to a variety of insights and responses to consumption. For example, we perceive certain shops and products as associated with one gender or the other. Marketers and advertisers use different techniques when targeting males and females. The color of the packaging, the environment, and the way sales personnel interact with customers are influenced by gender differences.[23] Women's motivations for shopping lead to different behaviors and approaches.[24] These differences and the implications of these differences are just as important to retailers as they are to marketers and advertisers. Our understanding of the differences between men and women in relation to shopping is limited, as very little research has been undertaken. To help understand a bit more about these differences, we discuss what we do know about how a person's social upbringing and how their biological status affects the way they shop.

Gendered Shopping Behavior

When women are depressed, they eat or go *shopping*. Men invade another country. It's a whole different way of thinking.

—Elayne Boosler, comedian

An American study found that two out of three women enjoy shopping, compared to only one in three men. Women rank shopping as their third most enjoyable leisure activity, after vacations and dining out, whereas men rank it last. Women feel they are accomplishing something through shopping, men don't.[25] This demonstrates that women and men have a different set of priorities, preferences, and attitudes that result in different gender responses, decision-making processes, and purchase outcomes.[26]

Male shopping behaviors have been studied,[27] and building on earlier findings[28] that although there are some differences in attitudes and motivations toward shopping, "the contrast between male and female shopping styles is not actually as marked as the expressed rhetoric would lead us to believe."[29]

Researchers did find that women were more positive about shopping than men; many men still view shopping as "effeminate," and men tend to shop for a purpose rather than "shopping for shopping's sake."[30] These researchers looked at common stereotypes of male shopping behavior, namely "Grab and Go," "Whine and Wait," and "Fear of the Feminine," and found relatively little support for the three stereotypes.[31] Males were found to engage in such "feminine activities" as alternative evaluation, bargaining, and bargain hunting, browsing behavior, enjoyment of shopping, and some admitted to "shopping like a lady." The reality may be that males and females are becoming more similar in shopping behaviors and what they want from the shopping experience compared to the traditional perceptions, which will have implications for retailers. Currently however, research shows that shopping is still considered to be a feminine activity.[32]

One study found gender differences to have a strong impact on the consumption-related attitudes, behaviors, and consumption orientations of the elderly.[33] Through the use of questionnaires, the researchers identified elderly women to be more price conscious than their male counterparts, perceive themselves to be more adventurous, have more market knowledge, seek discounts, be more deal prone, and enjoy shopping more.[34] This is an important first step in understanding what the gender differences are. However, it is limited in that it cannot generalize to age groups other than the elderly.

As women are becoming an increasing force in the car buying market, a team of researchers investigated their process of car buying compared to males. Females were found to differ in their attitudes and in the variables that were important to them in making the purchase decision. The genders differed in their attitudes toward price consciousness, expectations (belief about the future), functional ability, self image, satisfaction, and loyalty. Price consciousness was the only variable found to be important to both males and females; however, this was for different reasons. For males, the price led to higher expectations of the car and an ability to impress others, whereas females found it important as an assurance of quality.[35] The findings of the study suggest that the factors investigated were not as important to females as they were to male buyers. It could be that other variables found to be important in the car buying process, such as search behavior and satisfaction with car dealer, may be more relevant to female consumers.[36]

Males and females also differ in their purchasing processes. When studying the purchasing pattern of consumers in a mobile phone store, the urban geographer Underhill found that males preferred to gather information on their own from written materials and could leave the store without ever dealing with a salesperson.[37] Females were more likely to depend on the salesperson for information and required more visits to the store and more consultation than males before making the purchase decision. Through observational research, Underhill examined shopping habits of males and females, and provides some valuable insights. For example, males move faster through store aisles, spend less time looking and usually don't ask for help, whereas females want to be listened to, to be taken seriously, want to read promotional material, and think about it.[38] These gender-differentiated behaviors are relevant to retailers when they try to create successful shopping experiences for the consumer.

Biological Differences in Shopping Behavior

A variety of studies have shown gender differences in several areas relevant to retail. We now know that women and men are different in terms of the following:

- processing information[39]
- attitudes toward shopping
- motivations and responsibility
- responses to environmental cues (e.g., personal dress)
- needs in the selling encounter

Yet, many of the studies have described rather than explained the underlying reasons for these attitude and behavioral differences. At the same time, other studies have shown that making a purchase leads to outcomes such as positive emotional states and behaviors.[40]

Other research looks at gender influences on perceptions of the environment,[41] service quality,[42] the sex, and the number, and appearance of service personnel.[43] Yet we still do not know much about whether the sales approach or techniques should be different according to the gender of the customer.[44]

It has been established that men and women process information differently. For example, when looking at advertising material at point of purchase, a woman will take in all the available message cues. Men do not take in the same level of information. Men are more selective (if they notice the advertising at all) and more focused when assessing cues. Women take a broader scan of the store and can become irritated by displeasing aspects of the environment. A man may not even notice what is displeasing the women. As writer Cynthia Nelms has said, "If men liked *shopping*, they'd call it research."[45]

Another finding says that men's brains tend to be better at understanding and building systems; women's brains are better at communicating and empathizing. Obviously, there are many other factors such as the social environment that are crucial in understanding differences between men and women. The finding relating to empathic versus systemizing brains may explain why a man is keen to discover how a gadget works while the woman is interested in how the gadget will make her life easier. It may also explain why a man is happy to learn about the gadget by reading the packaging. A woman will want to talk with sales staff (or other customers) about the gadget. She is happy to share experiences and knowledge about the gadget. Women are keen to establish a relationship with sales staff whereas a man is happy just to complete the purchase transaction. Finally, it has been clearly established that, overall, women enjoy shopping a lot more than men do, which is just as well, as they spend a lot more time doing it than men.

Female consumers are powerful purchasers yet there is no substantive body of theory on how to target them effectively.[46] This is particularly true in shops that are traditionally considered male domains, such as hardware stores.

Where the American Woman Shops

The dollars spent in retailing in America are huge. It is estimated that over 3.3 trillion dollars were spent in American stores in 2007; and this number increases every year. The American retail industry has a variety of channels available to women. Catalogues, online shopping, farmers' markets, malls, and temporary shops are some of the many places where women can shop, thus retailers must assess in which channels they need a presence.

We spend on general merchandise, cars and car repairs, food and drink, home improvement and fuel. We have a lot of stores to choose from to spend the cash that we have, including the following:

- furniture and home furnishing stores
- health and personal care stores, such as hairdressers
- accessories and clothing stores

- sporting goods and hobby stores
- book and music stores

There are also general merchandise stores, electronic and appliance stores. We can shop in the mall, at the gas station, at outlet malls, in strip centers, and online for secondhand or new goods bought in an auction or online store. Consumer products are presented to us constantly and we are bombarded with advertising through print, TV, and radio. Often, we are given coupons that encourage us to stick with a particular brand or try a new one and to save money at the same time. Women have so many choices and the competition for share of wallet is fierce. Businesses that best understand and can meet the female shopper's needs will be rewarded.

The Structure of the Book

This book gives business students, executives, and retail experts a chance to understand what shopping means to the lives of the American woman.

The book is organized into a series of discrete chapters. You can read from front cover to back or select the chapters most relevant to your current needs. This first chapter profiles the American woman including the latest statistics available on education levels, employment, fertility, life span, the boomers, living in poverty, and personal wealth. The impressive power of women in the retail market is discussed, including women's decision-making, financial, and purchasing power, plus their loyalty and power of recommendation that can continue over generations. Then, the background to the data collection is presented (i.e., who we interviewed, their number, age range, and demographics). Finally, we take a look at the American retail industry and the variety of channels available to women. Catalogues, online shopping, farmers' markets, malls, and temporary shops are some of the many places where women can shop and retailers must assess in which channels they need a presence.

Chapter 2, Women and Shopping in America, contains a brief history of retailing. The origins of retailing are echoed through to today despite the many changes that have occurred. We include this brief history of retailing because in many ways the history of retailing is the history of women. As the role and power of women have changed, so has the retail industry and we look at some of these changes. The history covers early trade through to the development of the department store and down-town shopping districts following the industrial revolution.

Chapter 3, Women and Place, is particularly important as it explores the development of American retail as a place for women to be and to socialize. The importance of place for women is evidenced with the establishment of the mall. The mall, as a place for women, has had an extraordinary role in the development of the American landscape. In this chapter, we refer to several American authors who have brought to public attention the importance of place in the establishment and maintenance of contemporary society.

Chapter 4 is titled Shopping as a Life Skill. Here we introduce the notion that shopping is a craft that is taught, both indirectly, and deliberately by parents, particularly mothers. The marketing literature refers to this general area of study as consumer socialization and intergenerational influences when specifically referring to families. Understanding how women learn to shop is important to our understanding of the mother-daughter shopping dyad and can provide significant opportunities for highly focused brand campaigns.

Chapter 5 is titled Shopper Types. The findings from our research, including our identification of five distinct types of shoppers, are presented in this chapter. This chapter contains the result of our original research. Here we present the results to the question "Why do women shop?" Importantly, the question was answered by the women themselves. We have simplified the responses into a five part typology of shopping styles. Most women tended toward or were clearly identifiable as one of the five typologies of shopper. The following are the shopper styles:

1. *Ms. Grab and Go* is time poor, generally not fond of shopping, and quick and focused in her shopping.
2. *The Lone Browser* wanders the stores for many hours absorbing the latest trends in merchandise.
3. *Retail Therapy* shops for a boost to tired or distressed spirits.
4. *"Yo, Girlfriend!"* shops in packs, often spending weeks or months planning major shopping trips.
5. *The Hunter* is always alert, serious, and focused on finding a bargain or something unique.

We delve more deeply into each shopping typology and discuss the underlying motivations for the shopping behavior in each group. We discuss identity and creativity, power and independence, seeking solitude, emotional release, and companionship and what these motivations mean to the retailer.

Chapter 6 is The Shopping Experience and How to Improve It. The in-store and online shopping experience is the focus of this chapter. It summarizes what women love and loathe about shopping. Our goal here is to alert retailers, merchandisers, property developers, and manufacturers to the major dos and don'ts for women. The development of experiential retail has raised the standard of in-store experiences and presentation significantly for retailers, and we present some of the implications of what is sometimes called "the experience economy." There are many challenges for retailers when their store becomes a theater with the staff, the store layout and shop fitting, merchandise and the customers all being part of the show. However, this does not necessarily have to be daunting and we present a couple of case studies of excellence in retail. Retail is detail and it is so easy to get the simple elements wrong, which leads to unhappy customers. For example, poorly lit or cold changing rooms are not acceptable to many women.

What do women want from retail sales staff? We explore the customer and salesperson relationship and how important it is to the women interviewed.

The online shopping environment has to be consistent with the in-store experience and is becoming a critical part of the retail offer as women undertake their preliminary research online as part of the shopping experience. This is a crucial chapter for anyone in the industry, as using the typology we discuss what it is that women are looking for in a store.

Chapter 7 is called Implications and Conclusions. While we know more about why women shop, there is still a divide between those who are known as utilitarian shoppers and the hedonic shoppers (i.e., those who shop for a functional purpose and those who shop for pleasure and leisure). An understanding of these differences will assist many retailers and marketers in developing appropriate strategies. The contemporary American woman is so very different from her mother or grandmother. We wonder what lies ahead for the women of America and what they will want from retailers and property developers.

What changes will the new economic order place on consumption in general? How can retailers respond to these challenges? What technologies will be influential in retailing and what new channels may emerge? Will shopping remain a female activity or will a new gender balance develop?

Finally, the preparation for this book has been a great pleasure for us. It reminds us that retail is fun, great fun. Whether shopping as part of a daily routine or just for pleasure, women will always continue to seek out those retailers who will provide appropriate experience and products for them; we hope you will enjoy the reading of *Consumer Behavior: Women and Shopping* and we welcome your feedback.

CHAPTER 2

Women and Shopping in America

Any book about shopping for American women must consider how women's lives have changed. What are the differences between the lives of women at the beginning of the new millennia and the lives of their mothers and grandmothers? Indeed we really ought to start back with the "Founding Mothers" of America. What was shopping all about for them? Where did they shop? How did they shop? Was shopping an important part of their lives? Fortunately, books and articles written by American historians and consumer researchers can tell us quite a bit about earlier times.

In this chapter we present a brief history of women and shopping and how the nature of shopping has developed in Western societies.

A Brief History

The history of shopping can predominantly be regarded as the history of women. As one has changed or evolved, the other has reacted or adapted.

—Chuihua Judy Chung

Historian Paul Nystrom[1] identified five distinct periods in the development of American retailing:

- prehistoric American Indian trade
- the trading post period
- the era of the general merchant
- the rise and development of the independent single-line specialty store
- the "modern" period of the large scale retailer (e.g., department stores, mail order, and chain stores)

We know that shopping in America has changed significantly over the centuries as the facilities for consumption evolved and spread throughout the young nation.

The Trading Post and General Merchant Era

The early colonial period, from 1620 to 1750, did not have a formal retail system as we know it today. Europeans and American Indians were the earliest influences on the evolution of the American retail system. Trade occurred between three groups: farmers, artisans, and crafts people. Transactions at this time were simple, and people engaged in them to barter for the necessities they could not produce.

The development of a contemporary retail industry was effected by several elements including colonial regulations, estate duties, itinerant peddlers, trading companies, and specialist traders such as booksellers. The new mercantilist system permitted the colonies to trade only with Great Britain. This controlling environment severely curtailed the intake of import goods.

The colonists influenced the development of retailing by their reaction to the government and commercial interests. In the colonial period, up to 1796, merchants with mercantile associations, like the Massachusetts Bay Company, sourced products from Britain and owned company stores. The colonial merchants sold "clothing, fabrics, foodstuffs and supplies of all sorts."[2] When specialized artisans and craftsmen began to produce and sell goods to replace the European imports, the retail system we are familiar with today began. These first retail institutions developed as a result of the growth of local and regional markets and "the inequalities in the distribution of basic resources" to the far flung regions of the colonies.[3]

An important part of the development in retail trade in the 18th century can be attributed to booksellers. The bookseller acted as an importer and supplier of goods to the growing nation. Another key source of inventory for retailers during this time came from the settling of the estates of the deceased, which were sold by courts to pay estate duties. Yankee traders provided a wide assortment of merchandise, including clothing and household equipment, which contributed to retail trade in rural communities in the 18th century.

As the population grew and peopled settlements grew father apart, traders settled into communities and acted as both wholesalers and retailers, often selling small assortments from modest arrangements in their home parlors.[4] This type of retail format was closely related to the general store in the city—another significant American retailing development. General stores represented the "shift from specialization to non-specialization operations."[5] Also, "these merchants played a dual role as the primary conduit between customers and markets."[6] From the general store, the frontier store was developed to serve the westward settlements.

In addition to the general stores that served rural consumers, itinerant peddlers played a role in selling merchandise. In the late 1800s, there were over 10,000 peddlers who traveled from place to place selling a wide variety of goods such as lace, doilies, pins, needles, thread, and cheap jewelry. In addition to goods, the peddlers brought "gossip, news, goods, and services to even the most remote homesteads." This form of distribution lasted until the Civil War, but disappeared as a result of the advent of railroads.[7]

The role of White women during the 17th century was primarily that of wife, mother, and keeper of the home. Depending on the region, women's responsibilities were to cook, sew, do laundry, educate the children, and in some cases, produce goods such as butter, cheese, cloth, or ale for sale outside the home.[8] At times, women assisted their husbands in running their businesses, but rarely would one see a man assisting a woman with domestic chores. Whether Black or White, at this time in American history women had little time for leisure pursuits. In our research, we were unable to locate references about the role of African American women in the development of retail trade. This a story that we hope will be told one day to add to our knowledge of the role of women in the development of the retail trade in America.

The gendered role of women persisted until the mid-1800s when the Industrial Revolution took hold and resulted in the division of home and workplace for middle class, married, White women. Women's roles were redefined during this period to focus less on domestic production, which could now be fulfilled through manufactured goods, to a focus on the emotional and nurturing dimensions of family life.[9] The easier access of manufactured goods was very much part of the output of the Industrial Revolution.

The Independent Single-Line Store and the Modern Retailing Era

The Industrial Revolution in the mid-19th century facilitated the development of urban retail trade in the America characterized by a mass migration of workers to cities, coupled with the development of intracity transportation systems such as trolleys, that allowed people to move from one city section to another. This concentration of people, with disposable incomes, provided a ready market for mass produced merchandise. The self-sufficient lifestyle of agricultural communities was not possible in an urban setting, thus initiating the development of a sophisticated retail distribution system.

During the late 1800s, the department store emerged as a "one-stop shopping" destination, offering apparel and household goods to a diverse clientele. In 1848, A. T. Stewart's idea of a "department store" was put into operation in New York City. This shop employed 2,000 people and sold a wide assortment of manufactured articles. However, then, as today, New York City was much different from the rest of America. Thus, while it was possible to buy "imported luxuries" in New York, this luxury merchandise could not reach outlying areas until the railway system was built and marketing strategies were developed.[10] As discussed in *Counter Cultures*,[11] some of the earliest department stores such as Marshall Field's, Wanamaker's, and Macy's implemented new business tactics. These tactics included the encouragement of leisurely browsing, and the "one-price policy," which eliminated the need to negotiate price, allowing merchandise to be exchanged or refunded.

Entrepreneurs, such as Marshall Field and R. H. Macy and their retail establishments, made a great contribution to the development of American retailing. Together they helped to create more efficient operations, which helped to innovate and create many of the modern retail formats and concepts discussed below. Additionally, the new more efficient formats led to the abandonment of older retail operations like general stores.[12]

Chain stores were introduced about the same time as department stores. A chain store system is "a group of stores characterized by centralized ownership and control, and whose stores are highly homogeneous."[13] J. C. Penney and the Great Atlantic and Pacific Tea Company

(A&P) were some of the earliest chain stores. All of these developments took place at the same time as the role of women in society was changing.

The role of women as shoppers changed dramatically about the time that department stores appeared in the mid-19th century. Women were becoming educated and by 1870, over half of American women between the ages of 5 and 19 were in public schools. In the late 1880s, some women also began to attend college.[14] The cities, long "male-only" enclaves of business and pleasure, began to change when restaurants and teashops were opened to women. The extension of public transportation facilitated the change, and magazines such as *Godey's Lady's Book* encouraged women to make the trip into the city. The arrival of shopping districts in city centers set the scene for the creation of a female urban culture quite separate from the home. Women traveled by train to spend the day in town. The sole object of the trip was to visit the growing number of shops designed and built with their needs in mind.

The years 1890 to 1930 were a time of great change for American society. Attitudes toward consumption changed dramatically during these years. Previously, consumption had been seen as some type of awful sin. During the early years of the 20th century, it became good to want things and to consume. The consumer society had emerged.

At the beginning of the 20th century, women's roles began changing in earnest. Girls participated in primary and secondary education at about the same rate as boys did, reaching about 66% in 1920.[15] At the same time, about 8% of 18- to 21-year-old women were enrolled in college. Increased education and the demand for labor, which led to higher wages, attracted women into the labor force. The introduction of labor-saving devices such as washing machines decreased the amount of time that women spent on housework, making it possible to work outside the home.

While unemployment for women rose to about 20% during the Great Depression, when the United States entered World War II in 1941, the number of women in the workforce rose 50% to 19 million between 1940 and 1944.[16] About one third of the female workforce was married, setting the stage for the trend toward working mothers. After World War II, over 3 million women were forced out of their jobs to accommodate returning soldiers, but they often found other opportunities. By 1947, there were more women in the paid workforce than during the war years.[17] Increased employment opportunities for women created discretionary income and greater financial independence, which in turn led to occasions for shopping.

One major social trend affected women's roles and how they shopped. Between 1946 and 1961, over 12 million families became homeowners. This surge in homeownership was due in part to the benefits granted by the Serviceman's Readjustment Act of 1944 (commonly known as the GI bill). The GI Bill was a law that extended social benefits to returning war veterans, including unemployment benefits and the opportunity to qualify for low-interest guaranteed loans to buy a home (Home Loan Guaranty).[18] The move to the suburbs had begun, with Levittown on Long Island, New York, having the distinction of being the first suburban development in America.[19] At about this time,

> shopping took up much more time as domestic advisors urged women to throw out much that is still useful, even half-new, in order to make room for the newest "best" and to buy items that their mothers would have made.[20]

Urged by women's magazines to buy new goods to outfit their new homes in the suburbs, women did just that. To accommodate their needs, new retailing formats emerged and followed them to the suburbs.

Modern Retail Operations

Discount retailing can be traced to 1912,[21] but this niche did not begin to draw attention until the 1950s in New England. By 1962, E. J. Korvette was considered a leader in this industry, featuring a store in New York City seven stories tall, offering luxury goods like silk blouses and alligator purses at prices lower than department stores. The store operated three nights a week, while providing minimum service, all of which was unheard of at the time. The store had luxurious displays, chandeliers, and window displays, as well as international shoe departments, and fur salons. Other formats took the "no frills approach," which housed large amounts of goods piled in "distressed" stores offered at cheap, $10 prices. Most discounters however, chose formats in the middle of the two extremes, attempting to offer stylish merchandise at discounted prices.

Often the opening of discount stores caused frenzies, described as "circus"-like atmospheres.[22] One instance described a 1,000 car parking lot packed full, spilling into surrounding areas.[23] By the 1980s, the "Big Three"—Walmart, Target, and Kmart emerged as the discount industry leaders.[24] In 1980, Korvettes folded because of market saturation and competition from other formats, such as catalog showrooms and specialty retailers.[25] The tough economic times of the 1980s also took a toll on the discounters' maturing market.[26]

Toward the end of the 1980s, competition from alternative formats like hypermarkets, warehouse clubs, off-price retailers, and category killers forced discounters to examine alternative competitive strategies.[27] Many discounters began adopting diversification and differentiation strategies, which led to the rise of supercenters and private labels.

Supercenters, which offer grocery and general merchandise, eventually became known as the "Americanized versions of the European hypermarkets."[28] The supercenter has seen a great deal of success, which can be attributed to the integration of grocery selection into the traditional discounting format, which has forced many small grocers out of business.

The retail industry in America had become part of an international network that needed to compete well to survive. Currently, the fastest growing niche is the dollar store, demonstrating the sustained growth and loyalty to "value" retailing. Similarly, home goods stores like Sears's home improvement and The Great Indoors are also experiencing success as people choose to renovate or redecorate their homes rather than sell and buy up. Finally, much of retailers' growth strategies are focused on expanding overseas operations and successfully integrating the Internet into their current business model.

The history of retailing in America has been one of development and evolution consistent with the changing needs of the people, especially women. As women built homes in the suburbs, so the retailers moved to the suburbs and built malls.

The development of retail formats continues into the contemporary era. Outlet malls and power centers were created in the 1980s. Outlet malls grew as a result of manufacturer-owned retail stores needing a place to sell excess stock, while power centers were built to offer an assortment of big box and warehouse type stores.[29] The 1990s brought about entertainment and lifestyle centers. Entertainment centers feature multiplex cinemas, chain restaurants (e.g., Bravo's) and upscale, trendy stores. Lifestyle centers, similar in offering to the entertainment centers, "create a place to dine and shop where there is architecturally significant streetscape and building facades with street activity that make shopping and dining an enjoyable experience."[30] Lifestyle centers attempt to create the "small town" atmosphere that was once present in many American communities. In 2005, there were 48.6 thousand shopping centers in the United States, with a total of 6,060 million square feet of gross leasable area.[31] These centers generated $1.53 trillion in sales in 2005.

The retail industry in America developed with the nation, moving and adapting from itinerant peddlers to major investment in malls and department stores in the cities and new suburbs. This development of the American retail industry shadows the social and economic growth of the nation providing more and more facilities for the acquisition of consumer goods. In the next chapter, we explore the mall as an important "Third Place" for women.

CHAPTER 3

Women and Place

A place safe for human use for rest and recreation is crucial in any society. Traditionally, that safe place has been the home or a community facility. As the consumer society has developed and the traditional roles of women have changed, shopping has become an important part of everyday life, with most of it taking place in its own safe place—the mall. Today, shopping can be a purely functional activity or part of leisure. Leisure in contemporary America and other Western societies is regularly associated with shopping. We argue that for women, shopping can be part of leisure, sometimes as part of a holiday, or important time with family, sometimes a time for creative reflection, or for social, or individual expression. The significance of place and leisure for women in relation to shopping is a fairly recent phenomenon starting with the development of the department store followed by the 20th-century introduction of the mall. In this chapter, we look at how shopping became a leisure pursuit and how the mall became a very important place for women. We highlight the role taken by some merchants in the development of specific facilities for women. Facilities were designed to "seduce" the women into entering the store and remaining there to take advantage of the merchandise offerings. The importance of shopping to women was then recognized by property developers who purposely built malls for women to shop as part of their work and leisure. Over time, the mall and the role of shopping have taken on special significance as a "Third Place" for women, different from work and home. The concept of the Third Place concludes this chapter.

What Is Leisure?

Leisure is a residual factor; for example, it is normally seen as the amount of time left in the day after time spent on the following:

- *necessary time*: sleeping, eating, and personal care
- *contracted time*: paid work and formal education
- *committed time*: family and household responsibilities and unpaid voluntary work

Sociologists have found that leisure activities are now as important to the construction of identity as is employment.[1] Leisure is an essential component of our lives. It is a recovery time required for good health, for personal development, and for thinking about our lives and well-being. The amount of time for leisure varies by gender, age, and day of the week.

Leisure activities are linked to several crucial nonmaterial needs. They affirm social values, motivate healthy behaviors, and create positive identities. These are important factors for individual well-being. An individual may participate in any number of different types of leisure, for example, family and household activities, sports, or creative activities; or, one may go out for celebrations with friends and extended family.

Individuals can also participate in leisure as part of the wider community (e.g., festivals, cultural activities). The trend to use shopping time as leisure time is fairly recent, emerging during the 19th century, when shops were built in the middle of town business districts. Since then, major changes have occurred in how we spend our leisure time. For women, leisure is often spent in a Third Place, such as a gym, social, or educative gathering like a book club, or craft group like a quilting circle. Now we know that shopping is a very common leisure activity that takes place in the mall.

When Shopping Became a Leisure Pursuit

During the Industrial Revolution, a middle class emerged in America. Middle-class women were generally affluent, educated, and had access to transportation to the city center. This access to travel to the city created the notion of shopping as a leisure activity. The department store was a particularly successful innovation at capitalizing on this trend. It was designed for women by men who hoped to attract women shoppers and "*seduce*" them into shopping. During our research for this book, we came across the use of sexual references, such as seduction, to describe the relationship between women and the new department stores. The role of women in the development of the new consumer society was not all disparaging. Indeed, there is evidence that the role of women was crucial to the development of manufacturing industries in the modern nation. For example, women were often encouraged to use the latest forms of technology such as the so-called labor- saving devices for the home. There was also a belief that these new products and stores would free women from conventional restraints in the home and provide new opportunities for education and participation in civic society.

Department stores were a symbol of the new woman's mobility and acceptance in commerce and society. The early department stores provided cultural as well as consumer opportunities including reading areas, writing areas, beauty parlors, and even areas where one could listen to lectures on topics from economics to the arts.

One of the great department store retailers saw that women had an integral role to play in the post industrial society. Gordon Selfridge (1858–1947) was an American who established a new department store in London. He was an entrepreneur who knew he was bringing about major changes in retailing and is believed to be the person who coined the phrase "The customer is always right": "Shopping at Selfridges is a pleasure, a pastime, a recreation, something more than merely shopping."[2] He "claimed that he had single handedly torn down the walls of conservative British shop keeping and professed that his store was a modern public sphere devoted to the pleasure of ladies . . . He represented the department store as emancipating women from the drab and hidebound world of Victorian commerce and gender ideals."[3]

Shopping became a leisure activity and a way to meet people. Some retailers understood this and designed their stores and advertising to reflect that idea. Selfridge's department stores allowed women to participate in a wider social network. Gordon Selfridge did his own research when he was planning his stores. He went to London, to women's clubs, and to other stores to find out exactly what women wanted in a store. He claimed to be an active feminist working toward greater power and freedoms for women. Selfridge believed that he satisfied women and emancipated them. He provided them with a place for excitement and pleasure. The store not only provided the entertainment and the opportunity to be seen; it also sold the clothing that would be worn at the event: "Shopping at Selfridges has all the appearance of a Society gathering. It holds a recognized position on the program of events and is responsible sartorially for much of the success of each function that takes place."[4]

Shopping was seen as being part of a "cure," a rest break that would reduce stress and anxiety. He offered women the opportunity to treat themselves without guilt. The department store became a home away from home. Yet for much of the Victorian era, shopping was regarded as an activity that was immoral and indulgent.

By the 1900s, women could catch the train into town, have lunch, and visit a club or the theater. She was able to take her time browsing through the merchandise without her husband or children interrupting her thoughts. She could look at luxury items, enjoy them for the beautiful objects they were and not feel obliged to purchase anything. It is important to remember that when women shop it is not necessarily about purchasing. It is a mistake to confuse shopping with purchasing.

Although women were given the freedom to shop in the city centers, they were still seen as vaguely hysterical and not to be trusted. The French novelist Émile Zola wrote *The Ladies Paradise*, in which he viewed the transformation of shops and emporiums into cathedrals of pleasure, as immoral. He regarded department stores as sexual predators, determined to seduce the vulnerable women of late 19th-century society. Zola graphically presents an extraordinary picture of the early days of shopping in the cities as a place where women were tempted, courted, seduced, and entrapped in this consumer paradise. Women would be so attracted to these new department stores that their seduction was almost guaranteed. The store was a theater set for this sex scene with the sales area draped in white curtains to look like a bedroom.

In the Parisian store Bon Marché, women would be tempted into the stores and then by clever use of design, wall mirrors, and floor layout they would be trapped, unable to escape:

> What's necessary . . . is that they walk around for hours, that they get lost. First of all, they will seem more numerous. Secondly . . . the store will seem larger to them. And lastly, it would really be too much if, as they wander around in this organized disorder, lost, driven, crazy, they don't set foot in some departments where they had no intention of going, and if they don't succumb at the sight of things which grab them on the way.[5]

This store design tactic is the forerunner of the modern IKEA racetrack layout that forces customers to follow a predetermined path that ensures that they are exposed to all the merchandise. These early retailers certainly set a remarkable standard for the shopping malls of today.

For the last 150 years, women have gone to meet with friends and browse through shops. All-day shopping trips from the new suburbs became possible with the establishment of cafes and rest rooms in public places. Before toilets were installed in department stores, it was a matter of *if you can't go, you don't go out!* Most women had to travel long distances into the city and the early department stores understood that women needed clean, safe rest places if they were to visit the city. Women were anxious to get out of the house and into the city; and once the restroom facilities were in place, women of the late 1800s had a newfound freedom that was precious to them. It gave them a new place to be away from the normal routines of home and work. As the cities matured, the suburbs thrived and the shopping infrastructure followed the homes built there. The shopping infrastructure often took the form of a shopping mall.

Historians disagree on when the first shopping mall was developed. Some say it was in 1907 in Baltimore, when a group of stores created off-street parking, while others believe it was in California in the 1920s when supermarkets served as the anchor for a collection of smaller stores.[6] The first enclosed mall opened in Minneapolis in 1956, with regional enclosed malls and specialty or theme centers being developed in the 1970s. Regional malls are anchored by two or more department stores and feature 70 to 100 stores.[7] Specialty shopping centers often adapt historical buildings, target an upscale or tourist clientele, and feature casual restaurants. Shops at the Bellevue in Philadelphia, a luxury shopping mall, housed in a 1904 Beaux Arts building, is an example of this type of shopping center, designed to attract female customers.

Places for Women

People have always looked to gather together in places for social interaction. Traditionally, women have used social clubs, food shops, school committees, and churches as their social places. In contemporary society, women of all ages are likely to gather in the local coffee shop or mall. They gather in small mother–daughter pairs, in groups out for the day or as individuals hoping to meet someone to talk to. Young teenage girls are often seen together socializing in malls and there are plenty of shops for them to browse through. These places for social interaction are often outside of the home and are what Ray Oldenburg calls "Third Places." In his book *Celebrating the Third Place: Inspiring Stories About the Great Good Places at the Heart of Our Communities*,[8] the home is regarded as the "first place;" work is the "second place," with the social venue the "Third Place." Oldenburg says that these Third Places are "the heart of a community's social vitality," a place for connecting, making new acquaintances, reviving old friendships or just being. All these activities are of value to American communities as they strengthen a sense of belonging.

Traditionally, in the "first place" (home), a woman has several roles. She is the cook, the cleaner, the laundress, mother, wife, accountant, and chauffeur. Her freedom to be herself, to grow as a person and to gain new experiences is limited by the multiple demands on her time. Home can be a refuge for some; for other women it is a very busy place where little socializing or self-expression can occur.

Women may have a much wider range of social connections at work (second place), and opportunities for social experiences and outings during breaks or after work are greater (as long as she doesn't have to race home to get dinner ready). This "second place," the work place, is often significant for women as it takes them away from domestic chores, introduces them to new people, and gives them the opportunity to develop skills, make new friends, and gain financial independence. For many women, there are rewards in paid employment apart from the wage. Social interaction is one of those rewards.

This newly named "Third Place" focuses on community-based leisure and social interaction. For women, a visit to a shopping center can be part of the Third Place, regardless of whether a purchase is made because there are opportunities for leisure and socializing when shopping. The combination of shopping with social and leisure activities is clearly acknowledged by shopping center developers who carefully plan their facilities to contain a mix of food outlets, rest points, and meeting places.

What makes place important to us? People construct and inhabit places that make sense, and have meaning and associations for us. Different places have different meanings and acceptable modes of behavior. For example, while it is perfectly appropriate to be naked in a bathroom, it is not perfectly appropriate to be naked outside a bathroom. Places of worship are treated with great respect, shown in the ways we move, act, and speak within the confines of a church. Yet a playground is a place for boisterous fun for people of all ages. Place helps to define what activities are socially acceptable. The objects in a place form part of the identity of that place. People want to undertake activities in places that contain things that enhance that activity and provide a sense of meaning for those who use the place. The activities that take place in an empty room change dramatically if that room contains precious objects such as those found in an art gallery as compared to a room with basketball hoops and terraced seating. Objects define the activities that take place in a given space. A place is often identified by the activities that occur within it and objects and meanings associated with it. The objects present and activities occurring in the place must be consistent and compatible with the meanings of the place. Places are created, developed and changed to fit into the needs of the society. We construct work places such as cities and business districts; places to play such as Olympic stadiums and sports grounds; and places to rest like the extensive suburbs of our major cities. When a place changes, our relationship with and the meanings attributed to that place changes as well. For example, natural forest areas may be identified as protected for conservation and preservation, and thus the change in meaning will alter both the activities that occur and the objects that are in the area. Places can have multiple meanings and purposes. A home is a place of shelter and rest, but it can be a work place with the creation of a home office. Of course, a home also says a lot about who you are, what you value, and what your position in society is. The owner of a mansion communicates a very different message to others about their place in society than a person who is buying a simple unadorned home.

The introduction of the Internet and telecommunications has given rise to the concept of cyberspace. Places in cyberspace are very different from their physical equivalents. Cyberspace has given rise to e-commerce and online shopping. Customers are now able to perform the same shopping transaction in any of the aforementioned places (home, work, or Third Places) creating quite a different experience. For example, buying a book or CD online from Amazon.com can be a very simple and quick transaction. Yet thousands of customers still go to Borders to browse, see people, be entertained, be educated by the books, relax on its comfy couches, buy refreshments from the coffee shop, and watch people go by. These different objects, actions, and experiences make a physical bookstore clearly distinguishable from the online experience. Customers can stay at home and browse the Amazon website at their leisure and have their purchases home delivered; but many still prefer, at times, to be out and involved in the richer physical experience of shopping. People watching is fun, and can help us explore our own place in society and how we fit into that society. Merchandise is an artifact that can represent us in the world, allowing us to create alternate images of our homes and ourselves and to explore new ways of being. For example, in-store cooking demonstrations can lead us to different ways of eating such as cooking with a wok while displays might motivate us to change our wardrobe from gothic to trendy or to take up a new hobby or replace bitten fingernails with sensationally decorated acrylic nails. Many American women love going shopping because they can explore alone or with friends, spot new trends, drool at luxury merchandise, pursue the latest brands, and be treated with respect as a valued customer—all away from home and without the pressures of work. The women we spoke with love to shop when it is leisurely and enjoy having their own place to engage in it.

Shops and Malls as a Third Place

The need for social interaction in a "Third Place" is a significant part of why women shop. Most of our interviewees commented about social interaction as part of the shopping experience. Many women now live alone in suburbs, often working from home or in isolated jobs. Some are at home with young children, or are part of the aging population of retiring baby boomers. All these groups need social connection. Shopping centers provide many opportunities for reliable, safe, and interesting social connections. Women are able to get out of the house, meet up with friends, and talk with shop keepers and staff as a way of relaxing. The development of shopping away from the village or the central business districts of cities has had a profound effect on the lives of women as they no longer have "go to town to shop."

Originally envisioned as places for not only shopping, but also for community activities, malls replaced central business districts as shopping destinations when Americans began moving to the suburbs. The shopping malls of the 1950s and 1960s were long narrow strip centers with an anchor (major) tenant at each end. Fortunately, more thoughtful designers quickly enhanced the bleak designs. Very few shopping centers have managed to maintain the standards of the Parisian department stores. Fortunately, contemporary retailers appear to have a better understanding of the concept of Third Place and some have provided shopping environments that are definitely new Third Places.

Researchers have recognized that the mall is a Third Place of entertainment and leisure, providing a social environment for women and their daughters and a place to develop friendships.[9] One researcher found that malls have transformed from being strictly purchase sites to being centers for many activities[10] and experiences such as play and browsing.[11] These experiences at the shopping mall can create special memories that are held for many decades, as one of our interviewees shared:

> There was a little kiosk that we would always go to in the mall and get malted milk balls which are my mother's favorite. And, to this day, I can't see malted milk balls without thinking of my mom (age 32).

The future of shopping may well be more social, with customers looking for social interaction and experiences that cannot be found online. Places with great food and drink, good entertainment, and lots of spots for people watching will be successful. It is no longer necessary to leave the house to purchase most merchandise, so social contact will become more important to the in-store shopping experience.

As women's roles have changed due to education, emancipation, and employment, they have gained social and financial independence. From the barter system in colonial times to lifestyle malls and the convenience of online shopping in the 21st century, the retail system has evolved to accommodate the changing needs and shopping motivations of women. Much of that adaptation of the retail system has had a significant focus on women and what the retailers regard as being attractive to women.

CHAPTER 4

Shopping as a Life Skill

This chapter focuses on the acquisition of consumer and shopping skills through mother–daughter interactions. The acquisition of consumer skills is termed "consumer socialization" by researchers and occurs as a result of parents (almost always the mother) showing children how to shop, either by direct instruction or by observing their parents' behavior. Consumer behavior information processing skills are also transferred by interacting with parents in consumption situations. These forms of direct and indirect instruction lead to the child being able to act as a consumer on his or her own.[1] While parental influence on consumer socialization tends to diminish as children get older, their influence on adult buying behavior is still important.[2] Faith Popcorn and Lys Marigold (2000) had, as one of their "truths" for marketing to women, "This Generation of Women Consumers will Lead you to the Next."[3] This quote highlights the very strong connection between one generation of women and the next in relation to shopping and consumerism.

Of course, it is our mothers who give us life and protect us in our early years. It is our mothers who provide us with food and shelter and lay down values and perceptions that last throughout life. Whether we love vegetables or loathe them, it is likely that our experience of vegetables was part of our lives with our moms. So it is with shopping. Often, women's shopping habits and attitudes stem from shopping with their mothers. Mothers teach their children so much about eating, cooking, cleaning, shopping, budgeting, and managing cash from a very early age. These lessons can last a lifetime.

Marketers and advertisers know about our bonds with our mothers and use that knowledge effectively to build emotional connections with their brands. We can see this in Campbell's soup ads where a mother serves steaming cups of soup to her children. Other memories, such as the aroma of a freshly baked apple pie or a bowl of chili, can evoke very strong responses in consumers. Many cultures consider the value and worth of women to be closely allied to their skills as a shopper and consumer for the family.[4]

Learning to Shop: Mother and Children Shopping

The intensity of the link between women, children, and shopping is so powerful that it is surprising that there has not been more research into the topic.[5] In this section, we summarize existing research on mothers and shopping and the transfer of shopping skills. One recent study analyzed data to develop a typology of six "mom" segments.[6] The typology aligns mothers according to their values and perceptions of their roles as mothers in relation to consumption and shopping. This study looked at how different women saw and responded to the market interaction with their children and shows how mothers and daughters exchange information, influence, and decision-making processes. Mothers were segmented into six distinct groups. Three segments are "marketing receptive," meaning that these *mom segments* readily accept outside influences on their children (Balancer, Nurturer, and Diva); three segments are "marketing resistant," meaning that these moms do not like outside marketing messages (Protector, Struggler, and Stoic).

The Balancer (25.4% of the U.S. population) generally has a reasonable disposable income, is working, and is committed to teaching her children about spending by giving them the opportunity to consume and to make buying mistakes.

The Nurturer (9.6% of the U.S. population) is an absolutely committed mother and her life revolves around her children and family. She is self sacrificing and will often go without as she saves money to be able to indulge her children.

The Diva (7.2% of the U.S. population), as the name suggests, likes to be the center of attention. She is very fashion and image conscious. Her children, dressed in fashionable apparel, can be part of that image. She seeks an easy life with her children and will give them what they want rather than manage a conflict.

The Struggler (21.6% of the U.S. population) works hard to live within her means, but is often unable to fulfill her children's requests because of financial constraints. She can resent the media for highlighting consumables that she cannot afford to give to her children.

The Protector (21% of the U.S. population) is the mother who resents the external influences on her children from the media, marketing, and advertising because she sees them as undermining her authority. She actively teaches her children to shop as part of giving them a life skill. She is a disciplined shopper and only purchases what she needs. She is responsible, well educated, and often conservative.

The Stoic (15.1% of the U.S. population) is very conservative and makes her decisions very carefully. Often of a migrant background, her values lie with a paternalistic family hierarchy. This group is overrepresented in careers like information technology. She is not as close to her children as the other segments and can be socially or culturally isolated.

The study is useful for researchers and marketers as it contributes to an understanding of the various types of American mothers and how they might respond to marketing efforts. It articulates some of their core values and how those values are operationalized and transmitted to their children.

Studies that explore parent–child shopping have focused primarily on parental interactions with young children[7] or adolescents.[8] When shopping for clothing in early childhood, parents (primarily mothers) play a more active role in shopping than children do, and most parent–child shopping interactions are collaborative rather than unilateral.[9] One study that examined preadolescent apparel purchasing behavior[10] found that consumer socialization begins before adolescence. Between the ages of 8 and 12, most children shop with their mothers for clothing. However, children do influence their parents about what they buy. In particular, they let their parents know what clothing styles conform to what their friend and peers are wearing. The motivation to conform to peer groups begins at a relatively early age. Not surprisingly, as children reach adolescence, they are more likely to shop with friends at the mall and use shopping as a recreational activity. However, parents still have an influence on more expensive apparel items, such as coats, while peer influence is dominant for less expensive apparel such as tee shirts. It is interesting that preadolescents report quality, defined as long lasting and durable, as the most important purchase criterion for apparel. This emphasis is evidence of parental influence on purchase behavior.[11]

More recently, one researcher[12] found that mothers and adolescent daughters have different motivations for consuming. Mothers have a greater economic and functional motivation, while daughters' motivation is more self-expressive and focused on conspicuous consumption.[13]

Knowledge about the mothers and their attitudes to shopping and the transfer of skills and values focuses to a great extent on adolescents and teenagers. There are a few studies of adult daughters and their mothers, but these concentrate on college students. From these studies we find empirical evidence that the lessons transferred from mothers to their daughters, at least for apparel shopping, are long lasting ones. There are similarities between mothers and college-age daughters on their attitudes toward buying from secondhand stores, rummage sales, and department stores.[14] Both mothers and daughters indicate that they are equally satisfied with their clothing wardrobe, revealing the long lasting impact of consumer socialization. It is clear that daughters are not mere puppets of their mothers' influence. Mothers and daughters in this study differed on a number of shopping behaviors, with mothers shopping more frequently through mail order, specialty, and off-price stores than their daughters, while daughters shopped more at discount stores.

However, we do not know much about the influence mothers have on their daughters' shopping attitudes, habits, and behaviors later in life. The lack of research that examines the mother–daughter shopping relationship and the intergenerational influence in later life stages has been acknowledged by other researchers.[15]

In the next sections, we summarize and integrate the results of our interviews with mothers and daughters, of all ages, from across America. We asked them who they shopped with and why, and found that many of them were cognizant of the influence of their mothers on their own shopping habits, likes, and dislikes. This study is one of very few undertaken into mothers and daughters and their consumption habits, although the need for this work has been acknowledged by academics for some years. According to one study, adolescent girls see the experience of the mall as much more than consumption:

Do moms view going to the mall with their daughters as an opportunity to bond? How do moms view their role as a clothes-shopping companion? Mall management and retailers with insights into the mother–daughter shopping relationship could more effectively market to young girls and their moms. In addition, further research on mother–daughter shopping dyads could examine intergenerational influences in the context of mall behavior, and clothing purchases.[16]

The study of how mothers teach their daughters shopping skills and how they shop together throughout their lives is of particular relevance to retailers and mall managers seeking a greater understanding of this shopping relationship. Knowing how the mother regards shopping, children, and consumerism is critical to understanding how the daughter may or may not accept these values, indeed to consciously or subconsciously embrace the values as her own throughout her life. It is important to understand how young people learn how to shop, as

at least some patterns of adult consumer behaviour are influenced by childhood and adolescent experiences, and that the study of these experiences should help us to understand not only consumer behaviour among young people, but the development of adult patterns of behaviour as well.[17]

We found that mothers impart lessons on money management and frugality. Further, we found that shopping serves as a platform for daughters to launch their financial and decision-making independence. Finally, our interviews show that mothers and daughters often become lifelong shopping partners who ultimately influence one another.

The Gaining of Financial and Budgeting Skills

Being able to locate the best value for money is a life skill that can lead to an enhanced quality of life for generations of families. Each increase in purchasing power in a family can result in enhanced food and diet regimes, better health, increased longevity, and more secure retirements. Ways of shopping are communicated through the family unit, especially the mother. Family values are transmitted from one generation to the next and their communication may be effective or counterproductive, remembered or discarded, utilized or ignored. We know that it is from within the family that children and adolescents learn about shopping. Mothers teach their children to become consumers by taking them shopping as they grow up, by setting an example by what they purchase (or don't), or a combination of these. In this process, they convey to their children good or poor money management. Lessons in frugality and being a responsible consumer are often consciously taught. One adult daughter shared this memory of her mother: "She'd take me to the grocery store and she would try to make me figure out like when things were on sale, how much it was for each thing and how much money I would save." (age 28)

As we have seen in the current economic recession, careful financial management is vital to weathering economic downturns and maintaining one's lifestyle; thus, teaching children how to spend within one's means is a critical life lesson. It appears that one of the ways that adolescents learn about pricing is driven by parental nagging about purchase prices. Older adolescents seem to have more accurate pricing knowledge than younger adolescents as a result of family communication, such as parental complaining about the price of particular items.[18] A recent study found that adult children who had deal-prone parents were more likely to seek deals themselves.[19]

In our interviews, many women talked about early life lessons in spending wisely and the influence their mothers had on them. One young woman (age 26) we spoke with had learned the skills of shopping from her single mother at a time when there was very little money available for them. Her mother was a regular at garage sales and planned their Saturday outings carefully and was able to acquire good secondhand merchandise at low prices. For example, shopping at thrift stores (nontraditional retail outlets) framed this participant's memories of childhood rituals:

Like, my mom would get up on a Friday morning, and she'd have our map, and she'd circle the rummage sales that we were going to, and map out which ones we were going to first, and then she'd get our coffee, jump in the car and we're all going to these rummage sales, and the highlight of the rummage sales for us was the toys that were cheap and getting snacks 'cause sometimes they'd sell baked goods, and so that was something that we always did. Now, as time progressed, my mom doesn't rummage sale any more, but that was our whole childhood, and we got compliments in high school like, "Oh, that's nice." And nobody ever knew we shopped at the Goodwill or rummage sales. They always thought we lived like in Grand Blanc, not in Flint, in the city, so, I guess I learned it from her. I never thought about that 'cause she would map out like the places we would go, she'd have her little map, it's early in the morning, she has our coffee, and we're in a car just rummage saleing (age 26).

These skills became ingrained. She said proudly that she now almost never pays full price for goods and is committed to making price comparisons. She plans her shopping trips several days in advance. She reads the Sunday papers and circles what stores are having a sale of merchandise that interests her. She makes a list of what she wants to buy. Not only does she plan what shops she will go to, but also she plans her route through the store. For example, in Target she always goes to the clearance aisle first. Her carefully planned and executed shopping extends to regular household shopping as well as gift buying and purchasing paid for by her workplace. She is committed to getting the very best price for what she wants and loves the thrill of gaining the best bargains and being able to dress in a fashion-conscious wardrobe. We see that many of her shopping habits are directly linked to her mom's carefully planned and executed rummage sale shopping when our interviewee was a child.

Several interviewees disclosed how the early mother–daughter shopping experience transfers values from one generation to the next. For example, despite the fact that she is now affluent, one respondent reminisces about price-consciousness and shopping at thrift stores:

Okay. My mother was raised in the Depression, and so from what I can gather, people who were raised in the Depression, went without a lot of stuff, so one of their big prides in life later, is to be able to go and buy what they want, so one of her friends who was also raised in the Depression, told me about this place in Los Angeles that's right outside the airport, and it's called "The Place," that is a resale shop, but it's a resale shop of Beverly Hills socialites and movie sets and, you know, they get rid of stuff. So I went, and my mother was just absolutely mortified that I went to this place. She says, "I can't believe you're shopping Goodwill." Well, no, it's not Goodwill, and I bought, among other things, a red leather trench coat that was the most, up until that time, the most I had ever paid for a coat, which is $700, which under ordinary circumstances, $700 is a lot of money for a coat (age 50).

One dimension of being financially responsible requires seeking product information before buying to make sure the purchase decision is wise. We heard many examples of adult women remembering how their parents would search for information for major purchases. These lessons remain with the daughters, although the methods might change. One woman related how her parents' search habits influence her even now:

My parents shop around, clearly for them Internet was not available for them to do research, but, I mean, they always shopped around. They never purchased the first item they saw. They would shop around for price, and they would read the newspaper ads and newspaper articles about a product. So, in my case, it's something I have developed, but something I have seen from them as well. I do it probably at a different level than they have just because of the times are different but the concepts I think, are sort of the same (age 46).

Even when their daughters have better financial circumstances than their mothers, these lessons appear to endure. Daughters who have been taught to be frugal and search carefully for the best value retain these lessons.

Case Study in Budgeting: Clipping Coupons

Shopping on a low income requires careful research and planning. Early in her stay in America, Stella noticed women walking down store aisles clutching pieces of newspaper. I wondered what that was all about and one day while I was in a store, I started to chat with a woman who was concentrating on making sure that the item on the shelf was the item listed in the newspaper. It turns out that I was beginning to discover the world of coupon shopping.

Later on I learned that coupon shopping is a very important part of the American culture and that an industry of coupon sellers, advertisers, organizers, and promoters exists. One woman told me that working carefully with coupons was her way of contributing to balancing the household budget. She took great care to get the maximum benefit from her coupons and spent some hours every week filing them, checking expiration dates, and making shopping lists for the coming week. I was impressed, as we have nothing like the coupon system in Australia. It is a "win–win" marketing strategy that enables shoppers to make some savings and allows manufacturers to promote or introduce new products.

Pat clearly remembers her own mother as a "coupon clipper." She would accompany her mother on the weekly grocery shopping trips and her mother would have the coupons ready. "I learned that we used coupons only for regularly purchased items. Coupons did not influence our shopping list."

Declaring Independence

Ideally, as time passes, the transfer of shopping skills from mother to daughter results in the daughter being able to make her own decisions and become an independent shopper. Eventually, friends replace the mother as an influence. Research shows that this process begins early; children as young as 8 go to the mall with friends, buy merchandise independently of their parents, and indicate that their friends influence what clothing they buy.[20] Sometimes, breaking free of a mother's influence can create an internal struggle—stay with the inherited values or shift to one's own. For one respondent, her mother's shopping excursions to thrift shops transferred the value of frugality, which remains a part of her identity. This frugality is a pragmatic control mechanism for living within her budget. She continues in this vein, stating that while this behavior has remained a part of her identity, she struggles to resist it, which signals a desire to be independent of her mother's influence:

> Now I have to resist from stopping at rummage sales. Like, I want to so bad when I'm with my mom. I can't, and so I saw this thing one day, I said, "Oh, stop," and I was like, "No, keep going," so I resisted doing that I think mainly 'cause I don't carry cash, no extra cash, but I could see myself doing it one day, but I haven't done it yet (age 26).

One facet of establishing one's independence is the acknowledgement of and reflection on personal values. Resistance to the way "mother did things" is a way to assert one's independence, as reflected in this quote by a middle-aged woman:

Now, one of the things that I used to do that I don't do so much anymore, is something that I got from my mother, and I figured out it was a really bad habit. My mother was very much into quantity because she didn't have a lot when she was growing up, so if it was on sale, she would say, "Oh, this'll make a cute little change." Of course, half the stuff never got worn, 'cause it was junk, and so I had found myself doing that, "Oh, this'll make a cute little change," but then later I figured out, instead of having lots of "cute little changes" that you really won't wear, maybe you should have something that just knocks your socks off, so I tend not to do the cute little changes as much (age 50).

Daughters often see their mothers as "the pocketbook" that pays for the daughter's clothing and accessories, but this view diminishes as daughters grow up. Eventually, they want to fund their own shopping excursions. There is a sense of pride in managing one's money well and being independent. One of our interviewees said proudly that "I think it is more about finances, shopping by myself is the independence . . . as it is kind of empowering . . . I had my mom's credit card from a very young age. I was very responsible with it, not frivolous, and that may have been part of it, as the empowerment, and the independence of it" (age 39).

The theme of using shopping as a means of gaining and expressing financial independence was apparent. This resulted in a sense of pride, as summarized by two women: "I want to feel like I don't need my parents to do that, I can take care of it. I'm doing okay so I don't need them to buy those things for me" (age 27). In addition,

It gives me a sense of independence, like, oh yes I have my own money, I can buy whatever that my pockets allow and it's like you feel more confident, like I like this because I like it and I bought it. So I'm going to wear it and I'm proud. So it's a good feeling (age 21).

In addition to fostering financial independence, developing independent decision-making skills in children is critical and can begin at a very early age. For example, after her 3-year-old daughter refused to wear clothing her mother selected for her, the mother began to give her daughter a voice in the decision-making process. The mother stopped making unilateral decisions about apparel and became partners with the daughter in the decision-making processes of shopping: "After I had the first, she refused to wear that, that, that, and that, now I try to include her in as much of the decision making as possible" (age 30).

Many of our interviewees were in their early 20s or mid-life. These two life stages are where identities are "re-made with some aspects being confirmed, others denied, and new facets added."[21] For some daughters, trust in their mothers led to independence. They trusted their mothers to be aware of and fulfill their wants and needs, to the best of their ability. In turn, this trust led to confidence in one's own decision making. As they grow up, daughters tend to reject their mothers' opinions and decisions in favor of their own, in an attempt to construct their own identity. While this rejection can lead to conflict, the data from our interviews did not uncover this. Our results showed that shopping can be a safe place to display one's independence. As we see, shopping provides a context for daughters to gain independence. During childhood, parents, primarily mothers, provide their children with opportunities to exercise independence through making purchases.[22]

Shopping Together: Mother and Daughter Purchase Pals Influence Each Other

Mothers play a more active role in the consumer education of their children than fathers do, and coshop more often with daughters than sons.[23] During their lifetimes, mothers and daughters share knowledge of budgeting and of bargaining; they seek value and quality in merchandise, and they learn and understand the routines and rituals of retail shopping. As a result, the shopping habits, product and store preferences, and techniques are communicated across generations. This influence in the shopping relationship is not uni-directional. Daughters also influence their mothers, and grandmothers influence their granddaughters; this cycle of influence is called "reciprocal socialization."[24] A recent *Weekend*

Today Show segment highlights this lasting influence. A young bride, who was to be wed in a TJ Maxx store, said, "I learned the value of a dollar. I can see my mother, my grandmother, and my aunt here [shopping at TJ Maxx]."[25]

We found evidence of the generational transfer of knowledge, as one mother discussed how she shopped with her mother and how she, in turn, is teaching her 2-year-old daughter to be a shopper:

INTERVIEWER: With your mother, what age do you sort of remember best doing that with her?

RESPONDENT: Probably high school. And it was enjoyable and I looked forward to it, and we'd have lunch with my grandma. I don't know. It was just like a family . . . so it is kind of . . .

INTERVIEWER: And now you're starting to turn your daughter . . . into a shopper?

RESPONDENT: Oh very much so yes. But again it's always. we make, we kind of make an entertainment of it. We're either singing or playing or talking about items or whatever it is. So it's very engaged with whatever is going on around us (age 39).

INTERVIEWER: Generation continues it's fun, it's fun what a lovely thing to pass on, fun and entertainment.

Mothers actively or passively communicate their perceptions and knowledge of shopping. Depending on the mother these messages may be positive, negative, partial, or detailed in response to the value and personal characteristics of the mother. What we found in our interviews was that, for many mothers and daughters shopping becomes a lifelong partnership. Initially, this partnership revolves around the mother paying for the daughter's purchases. But, as time passes, the partnership evolves into an exchange of information and views and the establishment of the daughter's identity.

The importance of shopping in women's lives and identity is[26] confirmed by research. The majority of young girls reported that their peer shopping companions were "purchase pals." It is known that the vast majority (85%) of young girls went shopping with their purchase pals to assist with the purchases.[27] However, even though adolescents and teens often prefer to shop with their peers, shopping with mom is often seen as a safe haven and they continue to seek their mother's advice for important purchases. One of the benefits of mother–daughter shopping is the security that comes from trusting one another. One young interviewee reported, "I typically shop with my mom because we enjoy spending time together and I trust her opinion on what I am buying or shopping for" (age 20).

This next quote shows that, even for adult daughters, mothers' opinions are essential:

> If I am shopping for something that is very expensive, or something that I will have for a long amount of time such as a business suit or expensive dress, then I need to shop with my mom. High involvement clothing purchases, I need to do with my mom. No one else will do. I am not very good at making decisions, so I need her there to tell me everything. If I am shopping for cheap items that don't really mean anything, i.e., tee-shirts, then I like to shop with my friends (age 21).

In the early years, the mother guides the daughter with her purchases. Often the mother has to negotiate with her daughter from very early years as the daughter seeks to gain independence.

Train Them Young

The young woman who sees her mother as an ally in her shopping trips now has her own 3-year-old daughter. She is aware that her daughter is learning about shopping and the time out that it creates for mother and daughter. Another mother told us about how she sits in front of the computer at home with her 2-year-old daughter and shops:

> Shopping online we just sit together at the computer and I can pull up the pictures and explain to her how it's going to fit. You know, basically there's no snaps, no zippers, it's going to be very comfortable, then she chooses . . . then she'll accept it and chooses the color she likes (age 30).

This process provides the daughter with clothing that she can manage on her own, helps her to discriminate among merchandise choices, and helps the mother to make a purchase that will be used.

Children influence the attitudes of their parents and these influences remain throughout their life span.[28] Over the years, a role reversal often occurs. Research shows that reciprocal socialization continues into the later adult life of the daughter, extending even to influencing the decision processes of elderly parents.[29] We found that daughters offered information and advice to their mothers on purchase decisions. Mothers acknowledge that they use their adolescent daughters as role models and fashion marketers.[30] Often, a daughter begins to be a shopper for her mother. The following quote demonstrates intergenerational influence, where the daughter becomes a "personal shopper" for her mother:

> She's not really going for anything in particular and I become her personal shopper. I see things and "this looks like you, try it on" . . . But I just kick right into shopper mode for her, help her find, she likes Chico's so we'll go to Chico's and I can go and when I travel I go in Chico's and immediately pick up (items), this is her, this is her, send her a little package (age 39).

The maternal influence can remain even after the death of the mother. One woman whose mother had died years ago remarked that she shopped with her mom "*sitting on my shoulder*" (age 50). The importance of the mother–daughter shopping experience extends beyond feelings of self-worth resulting from astute choice making, and relates to the value of the mother–daughter relationship acted out in a place of consumption, and that the strength of the maternal influence is such that it may continue throughout adolescence into maturity and, indeed, old age. In this chapter, we have reported on the ongoing and powerful relationship that exists between mothers and daughters. It is a bond that transmits social and financial skills and preferences. This consumer socialization provides lessons that continue through the generations. Mothers and daughters shopping are critical to our understanding of shopping and are a topic in need of further research.

CHAPTER 5

Shopper Types

Women shop for many different reasons and the underlying motivations affect where and how she shops, who she shops with, as well as what (if anything) she purchases. Based on our interviews, we have identified five different shopper types, their underlying preferences, activities, and motivations. The shopper types are the following:

- Ms. Grab and Go
- The Lone Browser
- Retail Therapy
- "Yo, Girlfriend!"
- The Hunter

We must remember that these shopper types are not mutually exclusive. Depending on when and where she is shopping, a woman might be a Lone Browser one day and seek Retail Therapy on another; and life stage will alter how a woman shops depending on levels of disposable income and social contacts.

First, we describe each shopper type and provide illustrative quotes from our research. During this section, we discuss some of the major motivations for why women shop, drawing on the findings of empirical research in the United States, Australasia, and the United Kingdom. Our findings reveal that of the five shopper types only one, Ms. Grab and Go, shops purely for utilitarian reasons; the other four shopper types are motivated in a variety of ways from seeking power and independence, looking for social interaction, solace or relaxation, and seeking identity. These four types, the Lone Browser, Retail Therapy, "Yo, Girlfriend!" and the Hunter, look for a more pleasurable (hedonic) experience.

Ms. Grab and Go

Ms. Grab and Go is time poor. Generally, she doesn't like shopping and wants to get in and out of a store as quickly as possible. Shopping is primarily a utilitarian activity, a means to an end, that end being the acquisition of needed merchandise. She is a focused shopper and efficiency is very important to her: "If I have to go in I'm going for something that I have to pick up, something for the house, it is usually like on my lunch hour, it is a very quick trip" (age 25). In addition, another young woman shares her desire to finish shopping quickly.

> Okay, shopping, I enjoy shopping but I only enjoy shopping in the mornings like right when the mall opens because I like, I know what I want so I go right away. So I specifically, I don't know, I think of what I want before I go . . . I don't like to be there very long. I'd rather get in and get out (age 19).

Ms. Grab and Go does not like shopping with others, preferring to shop alone because it is more efficient and shopping with others slows her down:

> I don't like to take my time and wander through crowds and get annoyed with a lot of people . . . I like to go alone more than with somebody because like a lot of the times having someone else with me slows me down, because then they'll have to try on clothes and you know keep looking around which is fine (age 19).

Ms. Grab and Go has, what is called by some researchers[1], a utilitarian shopping value. This type of shopping value refers to an unemotional, task-oriented way of acquiring products. The utilitarian or "rational" shopper is interested in efficiency.[2] If we carefully read the quotes, we see that Ms. Grab and Go is driven to be an efficient shopper. She doesn't like to shop with others and wants to get in and out of the store as quickly as possible. The utilitarian shopper is likely to follow a shopping list and wants to minimize time spent in the store.[3] Convenience is very important to her. Because this shopper is time conscious, shopping can be stressful. She is happy when she completes her shopping list within an appropriate time and spends little time seeking information and browsing in the store.[4] Retailers that make it easy for Ms. Grab and Go to find what she wants will be rewarded with repeat business. The utilitarian shopper often reacts negatively to crowded retail environments,[5] bright lights, noise, and promotion signs, all of which are likely to slow her down and make her shopping trip less efficient.

Research has shown that the utilitarian shopping value is not related to positive word of mouth.[6] In other words, Ms. Grab and Go is not likely to talk to her friends about her favorite retailer, probably because she is too busy or disinterested. However, the utilitarian value driving Ms. Grab and Go has a positive influence on satisfaction with a store and this relationship is stronger for some types of stores (e.g., grocery stores)[7] than for others. Shoppers with high utilitarian motivations have higher store repatronage intentions and have higher loyalty than those who shop for pleasure (hedonic shoppers).[8] If a store meets her need for efficiency, a Ms. Grab and Go will come back again and again. Ms. Grab and Go can be a very loyal shopper; she does shop but wants to do it as quickly and efficiently as possible. Interestingly, this same utilitarian value has a negative influence on what is called *repatronage anticipation* (looking forward to shopping at a store in the future).[9] This makes sense, as Ms. Grab and Go does not really enjoy shopping; thus, no matter how well a store meets her needs, she is not likely to look forward to shopping.

The second category of shoppers enjoy the shopping experience for a variety of reasons including recreation, relaxation, social interaction, and seeking power and independence. These are the hedonic, pleasure-seeking shoppers.

The Lone Browser

At the opposite end of the spectrum from Ms. Grab and Go, the Lone Browser approaches shopping in a leisurely way. Shopping is a hedonic activity. She can wander the malls for hours, soaking up the latest trends. Having time alone is important for many women, and we found that going shopping was the perfect opportunity for women to have some time out by themselves: to browse, to look at merchandise, and to have a coffee, to be in the Third Place.

Similar to Ms. Grab and Go, the Lone Browser does not want to shop with others, but for different reasons. The Lone Browser is not focused on being efficient; she considers shopping to be time to wander, unencumbered by others. This is a quiet time for her. For example, she doesn't want to take her children with her, and is prepared to come back and take them shopping later in the day, but she does not want anyone to be with her during this quiet time:

Personally, I shop more often alone. I don't really need other people's opinions. I don't know how that sounds. I kind of, it's very rare that I really need other people's opinions and sometimes I feel like when I shop with my girl friends it kind of slows me down 'cause sometimes I may know what I'm looking for or other times, I just kind of want to go as I want without as much distraction as possible, so I tend to shop about, I think, 75% of the time or more by myself, so, yeah, that's what I prefer (age 23).

One mother refers to her shopping time alone as *solemn*, valuing the time she spends meandering through the store at her own pace:

RESPONDENT: I have a . . . I don't know . . . sometimes I view it as a solemn activity—an enjoyable solemn activity.
INTERVIEWER: Solemn meaning . . . ?
RESPONDENT: Sole . . . by myself . . . not as S-O-U-L but sole. Like I just need to get out and be by myself, and walk around and touch things I guess, in the sense of retail therapy you mentioned before, whereas I don't necessarily need to buy something but it is very comforting to me to go into a store and just walk around, because again it is that solemn time (age 39).

The Lone Browser can spend many hours shopping:

INTERVIEWER: So how long would you say that shopping lasts on a Saturday for example?
RESPONDENT: On a Saturday, oh my gosh. I could be all day if I got to the stores about, if I started shopping around 10:00,

maybe I'll shop and get lunch at about 2:00, and maybe head home then about 5:30 or 6:00 or something like that. Typical day (age 23).

We found in several interviews that, like Ms. Grab and Go, the Lone Browser is a very organized shopper; she may plan her shopping trip weeks in advance. The Lone Browser looks forward to these planned shopping trips as a fun activity. For example, Z (age 46) describes a September shopping trip:

INTERVIEWER: That was a purposeful shop to go, you planned it?
RESPONDENT: Yea, it was planned; it was planned for 2, 3 weeks and that was the Saturday I had available. So I knew I was going to be going there on my own looking at shoes and clothes for fall.
INTERVIEWER: Is that a fun thing?
RESPONDENT: Oh, it's a super fun thing.

She plans not only where she will go, but also what shops she will visit and what items she is looking to purchase. That level of organization and planning reflects her independence and control in her life. While there is a high level of planning, the Lone Browser can be an impulse shopper as well:

When I was planning it I basically go through my wardrobe and I physically, you know, just kind of go through my clothes and usually the way it is organized, my skirts together, my pants are together, my shirts are together, my sweaters are together. So I try to evaluate what colors I want to stay with, I tend to wear a lot of beiges, blacks, and browns, and greens as well. And then I like to just add pieces that coordinate with that. So basically what I do is . . . I go through my wardrobe and look and see what I have, that I can wear another season. And what are some things I don't want to wear anymore, I want to get rid of. And some I am not so sure about so they kind of go into a maybe corner. But then I kind of make a list of, I need brown shoes or I need a brown purse, or I need a beige shirt, a cappuccino colored purse, whatever it may be, I go through and list the things, like a skirt, pants, tops, sweaters, purses, a jacket, coats, you know whatever it may be. Scarf, belts, and then I kind of leave my list in the kitchen so it is kind of a thought process after I start writing things down because if something pops in my mind later or as I think through it, I am like okay I really don't need a belt this year or whatever, maybe I'll cross it off so it kind of gets revised during that 1- or 2-week period before I actually go out there. And then when I am out there it's just super fun, I mean I like to try things on and sometimes I find things that weren't even on my list (age 46).

The Lone Browser does not always buy things on her shopping trips. She loves to look, touch, and feel the merchandise. Sometimes simply looking and touching the merchandise is enough. For example, A (age 70), describes her weekly trip to a fabric and crafts store:

I mean, even if I don't buy anything, I go in there, 'cause I like to look at the decorations of the flowers and craft things, because I like to do different crafts and so that is the things that I look for when I go in there (age 70, talking about shopping at Jo Ann Fabrics).

In addition, another interviewee discussed how she liked the chance to interact with the merchandise:

But, so for me it is the active process. I get to walk around. I get to see, I get to feel the merchandise, I get to see, you know, look at the displays, whatever it might be. It is a very active kind of involved process. So I like that part because I'm not, when I do things to relax it is not a sit down and veg for a little while. I need to interact with things (age 32).

Unlike Ms. Grab and Go, many women really enjoy the shopping experience. For shoppers like the Lone Browser, the underlying motivation is called the hedonic shopping value. While the utilitarian shopping value is relatively straightforward and easy to understand, research studies show that the hedonic shopping value is complex, multidimensional, and serves as an underpinning for several of our shopper types. The hedonic shopping value refers to the pleasure-seeking, fun side of shopping;

making a purchase is frequently "incidental to the experience of shopping."[10] For example, the Lone Browser does not necessarily have to buy something to enjoy the shopping experience and she may enjoy vicarious consumption by simply interacting with products but not buying them.[11] Browsing has been pinpointed as the second highest rated pleasure about shopping (bargain hunting was first).[12]

For the Lone Browser, the hedonic shopping value explains their browsing for pleasure and escapism. Unlike Ms. Grab and Go, the Lone Browser views shopping as a form of recreation or as a time to be alone, as is evidenced in the descriptions of the solitary shopping trips that might encompass an entire day. She takes pleasure in just wandering and looking around in stores. The Lone Browser quotes indicate that she shops for the stimulation and self-expressive aspects of shopping, which are dimensions of the hedonic shopping value.[13]

Researchers have found that hedonic shopping values have a stronger influence on several important retail outcomes for some types of stores (e.g., satisfaction) than utilitarian shopping values.[14] People with hedonic shopping values tend to be more satisfied with stores that invite leisurely shopping (e.g., department store) than those that do not. For other types of stores (e.g., grocery), utilitarian values more strongly affect satisfaction.[15]

Shoppers with strong hedonic shopping values like the Lone Browser, are more likely to talk favorably about a retailer to others, giving them positive word of mouth.[16] It is noteworthy that the hedonic shopping value has a stronger positive influence on store loyalty than the utilitarian shopping value. Finally, the hedonic value has a positive impact on patronage anticipation.[17] In other words, a shopper like the Lone Browser, who is driven by this hedonic shopping value, is likely to look forward to her next shopping trip.

Retail Therapy

There are women who view shopping as a form of Retail Therapy. These women seek social contact and use purchases to fulfill their inner needs. Some use shopping as a way to deal with their emotions. Another motivation that drives the Retail Therapy shopper is the desire to relieve boredom or alleviate loneliness. This shopper is looking for something to fill her time; she might be a senior citizen or retiree. Shopping gets her out of the house and is a purposeful and fun activity.

For the Retail Therapy shopper, going out, browsing and buying objects appears, for some, to be an antidote for anger or sadness. There is something about the purchase and process that makes these feelings seem less intense. Using shopping to deal with anger was common. Going shopping after having a fight with a husband was a story often told:

> RESPONDENT: Last week I was pissed off at my husband. I was
> seeing stars. I was so mad, and I actually had stuff to do at
> home, but I got up. I got in the car, and I drove to Detroit,
> and I was gone all day long, and I shopped my way through
> Oakland County (age 50).
> INTERVIEWER: Did it make you happy?
> RESPONDENT: Yes. And I'm still, and it wasn't momentary because
> I'm still happy 'cause I didn't buy anything that I didn't love,
> well maybe a couple of things that I may have to take back,
> but for the most part, that was when I got that suit, that I got
> that suit I told you that I bought last week.

Not all women who use shopping as a form of retail therapy are angry. Some simply look at shopping as a way to de-stress or decompress from their overscheduled lives:

> Shopping, when I call it retail therapy like a lot of other women
> do, when there's a lot going on, and I need it. When I need time
> to unwind, I find myself even gravitating to stores and to shop,
> but just generally, it's just leisure, to go out and to find something
> nice. It makes you feel good (age 23).

Others, when they are having a bad day, will go shopping to try to feel better or build their self esteem or relieve stress. They might splurge on something; clothing was often mentioned:

> Yeah if I am upset about something or if I'm frustrated or I'm
> just having like if I have a terrible week at school I will usually go
> and get something to cheer myself up and make myself feel better.

It's just, I don't know for some reason shopping and putting on new clothes make you look cute makes me feel better about myself again (age 19).

For some, the act of going shopping is enough to relieve stress when facing problems, regardless of age. The next two quotes reflect this sentiment from a student and a professional woman.

Shopping is my favorite thing I would say. Shopping is a relief when I have a big problem or when I was stressed out. I don't have to buy stuff when I was shopping (age 20).

I think shopping can be therapeutic. It truly relaxes me when I am stressed out (age 45).

For others, shopping *and* buying is required for them to feel better: "I definitely find that I shop more when I am sad because having new things helps put me in a better mood" (age 21).

However, there are some product categories, such as bathing suits and jeans, which they avoid at these times, probably because the process of trying them on might make them feel worse: "I like to shop when I had a bad day and I like to find something nice, but no bathing suits" (age 19).

Shopping can make some women feel better about traumatic events such as the ending of a relationship: "I like to shop when I am down in the dumps or if I just broke up with my boyfriend" (age 20).

Often the Retail Therapy shopping trips were unplanned, and some occurred in the heat of the moment. The women who shopped for Retail Therapy tended to shop alone, although they might seek social contact during their shopping excursion.

Some women might not necessarily enjoy shopping, but prefer it to staying at home. For example, two older respondents, when asked what they liked about shopping replied,

I don't know, I think it is just something, getting away from the different things at home and looking at different things, just getting out (age 70).

And another septuagenarian remarked:

Okay I guess, it is just lots of times something just to go out and have something to do when I'm looking around (age 76).

Younger women too may use shopping as a way to occupy themselves and relieve boredom or loneliness:

I'm a graduate student, and I'm new to the area, and so I developed this shopping addiction almost, and I think it was more because I would get bored and so I'd go shopping. And I was just walking around, browsing around, looking at the clearance aisles, and then whenever I was lonely, like I had nothing to do, I'd go shopping . . . I think that shopping keeps me sane sometimes because I live where I work, and I don't socialize with too many people. I have a small circle of friends so they're all gone so if I didn't go shopping I'd be sitting here going crazy, so it's a kind of something to fill up my time, occupy my time (age 26).

Filling time and relieving boredom appeared regularly as a motive for shopping in the young and the older groups.

Usually when I go shopping, it is because I need something, or I am bored and I need something to do. So, what is better but to go look at awesome clothes and to make fun of the ugly ones (age 19).

There are several explanations for the Retail Therapy shopper's behavior. Retail Therapy occurs when a negative event (e.g., bad news, stress) is experienced, which results in a bad mood; to alleviate the bad mood, the individual goes shopping.[18] There are two major schools of thought about what drives the Retail Therapy shopper. The first is that she is driven by the need for *compensatory consumption*; this happens when "an individual feels a need, lack, or desire that they cannot satisfy with a primary fulfillment, so they use purchasing behavior as an alternative means of fulfillment."[19] In other words, shopping offsets a void in a woman's life. The second school of thought about Retail Therapy is that it occurs as a way to improve a bad mood, called mood-alleviative consumption.[20]

Research studies have found seven underlying reasons for Retail Therapy.[21] These include the following:

- positive distraction
- escape
- indulgence
- elevation of self-esteem
- activation
- a sense of control
- social connection

Positive distraction refers to using shopping as a diversion to forget the negative mood. Escape is physically removing oneself from the negative environment, while indulgence is pampering oneself or maximizing pleasure to reduce negativity. Elevation of self-esteem is using shopping to feel better about oneself. Activation refers to stimulating (activating) the shopper's senses. Retail Therapy as a sense of control enables the shopper to manage a negative situation and, perhaps, her emotions. Social connection indicates shopping to seek interaction with people, either by being part of a crowd or with sales associates. We found that our respondents engaged in Retail Therapy to escape, as one interviewee did when she was angry at her husband; positive distraction as one interviewee describes when she needs to unwind; indulgence as another mentions; and elevation of self-esteem depicted when we hear that putting on new clothes makes her feel better. None of our respondents tended to seek Retail Therapy as a way to connect socially.

The Retail Therapy shopper who uses shopping to relieve boredom seems to fall at either of the age extremes, either a student (age 18–22) or a retiree (age 65+). This form of Retail Therapy can be classified as a form of compensatory consumption. The term compensatory consumption is defined as consumption that makes up for a weakness or failure of some kind.[22] Thus, women might use shopping to make up for the fact that they don't have anything else to do, or that they are lonely or bored.[23] The act of going shopping may fill these voids for them and offer sensory stimulation through store design and atmospherics.[24]

Elderly women view shopping as a leisure activity that provides an opportunity to socialize and simply get out of the house, or sometimes get away from their husbands. In one study, two thirds of the sample of urban elderly shoppers indicated that they go to the mall for social reasons; respondents who reported that they felt lonely were more likely to linger at the mall: *mallingering*.[25] They value the experiential aspect of shopping, rather than the consumption aspect. Sometimes the elderly shopper is constrained by a limited income and has to restrict herself to window shopping. Shopping can be a pastime that keeps seniors mentally, physically, and socially active.[26]

At the younger end of the age spectrum, shopping can also be a way to relieve boredom. Shopping as a diversion for younger consumers (age 12–19) is the second highest shopping motivation among this age group.[27] While our respondents are somewhat older than this age group, we believe that their behavior is similar. However, while the elderly might go shopping to alleviate loneliness, one study found if a teen was lonely, she was less likely to seek shopping trips as a diversion.[28]

Similar to the Lone Browser, Retail Therapy shoppers who shop to relieve boredom often go shopping without buying anything.[29] She is different from the Lone Browser in the sense that shopping is not necessarily as enjoyable for her. The Lone Browser uses shopping trips to "recharge her batteries," but the Retail Therapy shopper seems to view shopping as a diversion.

Purchases made by our Retail Therapy shoppers tended to be self-gifts, purchased for personal use.[30] When shopping as a form of Retail Therapy, typically there are three popular categories of merchandise purchased: clothing and accessories, electronic products, and food.[31] However, it is interesting that while many of our Retail Therapy respondents mentioned buying clothing, only one mentioned food.

Previous work has shown that women shop (and buy) to lift their spirits or when they are angry at their husbands (as several of our respondents indicated).[32] Like other researchers, we found that shopping can lift one's mood.[33] Retail Therapy shoppers talked more about actually making purchases than did the Lone Browser. While none of our participants mentioned how much they spent on these trips, Retail Therapy shoppers tend to spend more than is typical.[34]

"Yo, Girlfriend!"

Ms. Grab and Go, the Lone Browser, and Retail Therapy shoppers are quite likely to shop alone. The fourth shopping type, "Yo, Girlfriend!" usually shops in a pack, is happy and relaxed, wears sensible shoes, and trusts her shopping companions. For "Yo, Girlfriend!" shopping is a social activity, sometimes encompassing entire days or weekends. Often, these women not only appreciate, but seek the opinions of others. They are also likely to share information with one another, taking on the role of a market maven.

The "Yo, Girlfriend!" shopper has not been extensively investigated and is a shopping type that calls for more scrutiny. Women shopping together are a major economic force, particularly when they travel interstate or overseas for days at a time as part of retail tourism.

One of the authors (Pat) has participated in "Yo, Girlfriend!" shopping trips for over 6 years to places such as Santa Fe. The size of these groups has ranged from 3 to 45 women. The larger groups require a bus. Women who participate in these shopping excursions have a variety of shopping intentions. Most approach these trips with a sense of opportunity. They do not bring a "grocery list" of items they want to buy. Rather, most have a vague "wish list" of things they might like to find. For example, on one recent trip with seven women, one woman was interested in jewelry, clothing, and home furnishings (in no particular order of importance). Everyone had something that they were interested in looking for, but no specific buying intentions.

Once in a store, group dynamics often take over. Some members identified items that they thought might suit another member and they make sure that person sees the item. When someone tries on an item (or contemplates its purchase), "Yo, Girlfriend!" shoppers usually serve as the audience and judge. During these store visits, the salesperson often becomes superfluous until the time comes to ring up the sale. "Yo, Girlfriend!" shoppers are more likely to seek out and trust the opinions of their shopping companions than the sales person.

The group synergy often results in increased sales for the retailer because girlfriends trust one another's judgment and are more likely to purchase when they are confident that the item suits them. In one 30-minute visit to a gallery in northern Michigan, a group of "Yo, Girlfriend!" shoppers spent over $1,000 on ceramics and jewelry and that was the first stop of the day. Frequently, there is no budget for the "Yo, Girlfriend!" shopper.

An important dimension of the shopping experience is the after-shopping merchandise display, often accompanied by a glass of wine. "That's half the fun," one "Yo, Girlfriend!" exclaimed during this showing of merchandise. Women want to show off their purchases and are egged on by compliments and confirmation about how appropriate the purchase is.

Generally women talk enthusiastically about shopping with their women friends:

> Shopping with girlfriends, that's I mean that's totally awesome. Because not only you're shopping, but then there is friendship, fellowship, the bonding experience in addition to these items you buy. So, when we go shopping it usually involves lunch or coffee or lunch and coffee. You sit down, you talk, and you compare things that you bought. And, because you are with people that have different interests, I think, and different tastes as well, you get exposed to all of these new things that you may not even be aware of (age 46).

Sometimes shopping with friends encourages women to "shop out of the box." Encouraged by friends, they are willing to try new things and are ready to take risks:

> When I shop with my friends, I can be a bit more risky or scandalous in my purchases (i.e., underwear, low cut tops, tight jeans, etc.; age 20).

Others love shopping with their relatives, grandmothers, mothers, sisters, and aunts:

> My shopping buddies consist of friends and my mom and sister! They are fun to go shopping with, they enjoy the same things I do and we love to find good sales or deals (age 19).
>
> My best shopping trips are usually when I go visit my aunt in Pennsylvania. My mom, sister, aunt, and myself all go to the mall around Thanksgiving or Christmas and try to hit all of the really great sales going on (age 20).

One woman indicated that she discusses with friends about items they are looking for. They look out for one another. They call one another if someone sees an item another friend wants (age 41):

RESPONDENT: I usually go with friends, so it becomes an outing. They usually come here because we can get on the Interstate, and leave their cars, and then . . .

INTERVIEWER: They, being . . . ?

RESPONDENT: Girl friends, lady friends. Yeah, people that enjoy shopping, and they may go, and I may go and not buy a thing. That's rare.

In one way, "Yo, Girlfriend!" is similar to the Lone Browser in that the shopping trip is not necessarily about buying. She often views these trips as a time to be together with friends or family, a social activity, rather than a time to actually buy things. One respondent (age 30) will include shopping, lunch, and maybe a movie as part of her time with girlfriends. She enjoys this time together, but it is a different type of activity to her preferred shopping alone for treasures:

Sometimes I will plan it out to go shopping and have lunch and see a movie with a friend, so there'll be a part of what we're going to do. So those experiences are more about spending time with that person, not about the shopping for me.

I often shop with my girlfriends. We will plan a day to go to the mall and go out to lunch, especially if we haven't seen each other in a while. This goes the same with my mother. We often shop together for an occasion, such as birthdays or holidays, to get the whole family done together (age 20).

The researchers' term for "Yo, Girlfriend!" is *social shopper*. However, unlike the other shopper types, there is not a lot of research that explores the behavior of the "Yo, Girlfriend!" shopper. We do know that this shopper type views shopping as an opportunity to spend time with friends and family, as a time to socialize, and an opportunity to bond with others. Social shopping meets needs to connect with others, labeled by psychologists as the need for affiliation. Women shoppers desire social interaction outside the home[35] and shopping provides this outlet. One study discovered that about 30% of women shoppers can be classified as "social shoppers" versus only 20% of men.[36]

Whom one shops with influences how one feels about the shopping experience. Having companions makes the shopping experience more fun for this shopper type. Shopping with someone else, rather than alone, results in a greater liking for shopping and a stronger hedonic value from a shopping trip.[37] Shopping with friends rather than family increases this positive shopping affect and value.[38] Impulse purchasing is more likely to occur when shopping with one's friends, but less likely to happen when with a family member,[39] perhaps because friends egg each other on when shopping together.

That women influence one another's purchase decisions during these shopping trips is not a bit surprising. This tendency to provide advice and counsel in the course of purchase decisions is called "Market Maven" behavior. A market maven is "an individual who has information about many kinds of products, places to shop, and other facets of markets and initiates discussions with consumers and responds to requests from consumers for market information."[40] Market mavens enjoy shopping more than others[41] and are motivated to share information because it gives them a sense of pleasure and enjoyment, or they want to help others in their group make the best decisions possible.[42] Women tend to seek advice from those they can trust, and it is common to see women emerge from dressing rooms, bypassing salespeople to seek the opinion of a friend. On a recent shopping outing with seven friends, one of the authors watched as her friends ignored the salesperson, and called to one another to "come and look" and offer an opinion. A favorable opinion usually resulted in a sale. In this type of setting, it is also common for friends to pinpoint items that they think would suit another's taste.

The Hunter

Of all the shopper types, the Hunter is the most competitive. She is alert, serious, and competing for that close out rack; she loves the thrill of the pursuit for the ultimate bargain or trophy. The Hunter is a serious predatory shopper. She is alert, assertive, sometimes aggressive and determined to get either the cheapest price or the most treasured item available. Often, the Hunter is committed to getting the best price she can for the goods she wants. They want to be complimented and admired for their purchases. For some women, it is a way of life, with one woman telling us proudly that she never buys anything if it is not on sale. One of our interviewees aged in her 60s is so committed to getting the bargain that she develops relationships with staff that allow her to negotiate the lowest price. She has no shame when it comes to asking for discounts:

> Now, this is, I really like this article, I really like this dress or whatever it might happen to be, but it's way overpriced, and you'll probably be putting it on sale. Would you like to check with the manager and see if he can do that now? (age 60s).

Most of the Hunters we interviewed were generous with information:

> I love getting bargains. Like people see stuff, "Oh, that's so nice. Where did you get it from?" And I'm willing to share, "Oh, this is only $10 at this store," you know. I went in and bought movies from Blockbuster . . . I wanted to watch a movie. Now if it costs $4 to rent movies, but you can get 4 for $20, so I'll just pay a $1 extra on it. I went in and bought it (age 23).

The Hunters we spoke to have a laser focus on finding the best price and are often opportunistic shoppers. One Hunter was a great researcher, starting her research with the Sunday paper. She bought the paper to see what is on sale, circled the items that looked cheap, and began to make a shopping list. Being an opportunistic and patient shopper, she will wait until an item comes on sale and buy in quantity and stockpile basic items, like the following two women:

> Okay, like I know I have to get my vitamins, maybe toothpaste, you know, kind of necessities, things that I need, actually I make sure I never run out 'cause I only get paid once a month, so I'll have like six bars of soap left, but let me get two more, and two more lotions so I never really run out of anything, so that's the need type of thing like necessities (age 26).

And, well, I really watch the bargains. Actually on Sundays I go through the paper and I write down the prices of different things and I kind of like. On Friday, it is right on my way then I can stop at the store and shop (age 70).

As an opportunistic and patient shopper, she is also willing to wait until a particular item, a one of a kind like a painting, goes on sale. While she knows that it may not be marked down, she is willing to take the chance rather than pay the full price. For example one respondent was redecorating her bathroom and said to us: "There's a picture that I want really bad for my bathroom, but it's $40, and I'm like, 'Hopefully, they'll have a sale soon,' so I haven't bought it yet" (age 26).

Finding bargains is a source of pleasure for the Hunter. She is always ready to take advantage of a bargain even if her available cash is very low. One day while shopping at Target, one Hunter found socks and house shoes on sale:

RESPONDENT: So I bought a whole bunch of those. I was pretty happy about that. It was cheap, but it was nice quality stuff, it looked like 75% off.
INTERVIEWER: So how does that make you feel?
RESPONDENT: Happy and excited 'cause I know that I'll need socks.

Making a purchase at a bargain price is often the end game for the trophy hunter. They want to get good value for the money, but the real win is the reduced price more than the object purchased. Taking pride in saving money and getting exactly what she was after is, in a way, the best of both worlds. She got what she wanted at a great price: a real win-win situation.

While the Hunter is generally price conscious, sometimes she will splurge if the item fits her needs:

If I can find a sale it's like, great, okay, yes a bargain. But I will go in maybe for an expensive jean because I feel jeans are like necessity. So I won't mind spending maybe about $100 to $150 on a pair of jeans because I know I'm always going to use them. Or a purse, like a designer hand bag (age 20s).

The Hunter will spend as much time in the store as needed to find the treasure, sometimes traveling up and down every aisle, especially the aisles with clearance items. She often knows the individual store layouts very well and has particular pathways through the store to make sure that she doesn't miss anything:

> In Target, it's weird. I walk in, and I go straight for the clearance aisle, and then I look up and down the regular aisles, I can go through, there's a clearance on the end, if I look at that, I'll look at everything else. Electronics, the clearance is on the end, most of the clearances are on the ends of the aisles, so I check all those, and then look at everything else (age 26).

The thrill of the hunt can be in winning the best possible price, but the pleasure doesn't end there. Many bargains are found late in the season and the articles purchased may be put away until the next year. For one interviewee, it was a treat to open her closet next season and rediscover the unworn garment, complete with tags: "Oh my gosh, I forgot about that, so it's exciting."

The reward for the Hunter is maybe a trophy garment or an object that brings pleasure and excitement into her life time and time again. It is in the nature of the Hunter that the purchase does not necessarily have to be new. Several respondents talked about finding wonderful trophies at resale stores. Using their considerable research and planning skills, many Hunters will actively seek out the very best of the resale stores. For example, there are resale stores located in affluent areas where a society matron would not dare to be seen twice in the same cocktail dress or evening gown. This need to constantly purchase new garments leads to an ample supply of excellent garments for recycling:

> So these women would give them these clothes that had been maybe worn once, maybe never. I mean, a lot of times you would find them with the tags still on. Fortuny designer gowns that were 3, and 5, and 7,000 dollars, I bought one, well about a year ago, and paid $75 for it (age 60s).

The Hunter is a strategic shopper, taking the time to build relationships with store sales associates so that she is able to gain preferential treatment in the store. For example, one is on first name basis with sales associates, so she can ask them to put items aside for her before they go on sale. This allows her to shop at her convenience, knowing that there is little competition from other shoppers and she will get the "pick of the crop" at the reduced price:

> I'll go through the store, and I'll say, "This I want for Senior Day, and this I want for Senior Day," and they fill me out a form, and then when Senior Day, when Wednesday comes, they just charge it to my charge card (age 60s).

Shopping can be a form of treasure hunt, particularly for those women looking for something different and unusual that helps them express the uniqueness of their own identity. The Hunter is looking for the win, but the prize is not always the best price; it may be that unique piece of clothing that no one else has, or as S (age 60s) tells us, the trophy was candle holders that she had been hunting that she found at a bargain price:

> I was looking for some candle holders, and I wanted some like 3 foot candle holders, and I went to a variety like bath and linen and bed kind of things, stores, and I needed three of them. Well, three of them, we were looking at about 150 bucks for those, and I thought, I wonder, I went into Walmart for something else, and "I wonder if they have candles in here or not." I found exactly the size, exactly the color, exactly the height that I wanted. They were $19 a piece, so I bought my three, so I'm off and running, and I was so proud of my purchase.

We spoke with one woman in her early 30s who finds shopping is a 'frivolous and carefree' time for her. It is a time when she can hunt for items from consignment stores as a fun activity. She will also hunt at mainstream stores, particularly in the end of line and sale racks. There is not necessarily a shopping agenda in mind on the treasure hunt:

> INTERVIEWER: Okay. So, did you hunt for Banana Republic?
> RESPONDENT: I did. I love their sales racks, I love seeing if I can find something that maybe there aren't 15 of them sitting on

the rack, they might be a one-of-a-kind kind of thing that probably just means that everyone bought up all the other ones and that's the only one left, but I feel like I've found a treasure in amongst everything else, so yeah.

INTERVIEWER: And that makes you feel really good?

RESPONDENT: It does, yeah.

INTERVIEWER: Because it's a hunt and it's a treasure.

RESPONDENT: M'hm (age 30s).

Some Hunters will visit favorite stores just to see what is available: "Okay, we like TJ Maxx and Marshalls, so we might start there, see what bargains we can find" (age 20s).

Several motives underpin the Hunter's behavior. Her quest for bargains is a source of excitement and gives her a sense of accomplishment. She bargains because she perceives that list prices are too high and she wants a *fair* price for what she buys. Finding a bargain or a treasured item provides an opportunity to show off the fruits of her labor.

There is something exhilarating about finding a great bargain, so we were not at all surprised by the detailed accounts we heard about this topic. In fact, looking for and finding bargains is yet another dimension of the hedonic shopping motivation and is identified as one of the shopping experiences that gives women the greatest enjoyment; nearly 80% identify this as a "thrill."[43] Acquiring bargains increases the sensory involvement during the shopping trip and provides excitement.[44] The Hunter's behavior can be explained by assertion theory, which suggests that people strive to achieve and seek success and admiration.[45] In this case, women are admired for their shopping achievements, such as getting a great price or a unique piece of merchandise. Several of our Hunters told us that they felt a sense of accomplishment when they found a great item at a great price; this feeling can be categorized as ego expressive, meaning that it makes the "finder" feel good about herself.[46]

Some Hunters like to bargain as a part of the shopping experience and take much pride in their negotiation ability. This "pleasure of bargaining" has been identified as a primary shopping motivation.[47] We heard more than one Hunter from our sample say that she bargains because she thinks that merchandise is overpriced and further, she knows that the merchant will be taking markdowns in the future. So, it is in her best interest to bargain now to see if she can get the desired item now rather than later. Research shows that when consumers perceive that merchandise is over-priced, they are more likely to bargain.[48] Of course, for the Hunter's bar-gaining strategy to be successful, the merchant, or salesperson, must be willing to engage and have the power to do so. This is more likely to hap-pen with smaller, independently owned businesses, although one Hunter was particularly skilled at negotiating with salespeople at national depart-ment stores. As with other successful negotiators, the Hunter is willing to walk away if she does not get the price that she wants. She is also patient, in some instances returning to the store again and again while she waits for the markdowns to come.

The desire to show off the outcome of the shopping experience with others is another facet of market mavenism. The Hunter loves to share information and to show off her trophies. We can see an example of this sharing behavior on YouTube (*The Haul*). *The Haul* is a series of uploads to YouTube that offer a narrated overview of recent shopping sprees. These uploads provide a forum for (primarily) young women to "show off the fruits" of their shopping trips.[49] These narratives do not always focus on price, but rather highlight products they are passionate about. For example, "juicystar07" recently posted a narrative about purchasing jeans from Forever 21 and had over 700,000 views of this posting.

Finally, the Hunter often seeks unique, one of a kind, merchandise that is not necessarily a bargain. The fact that the item is either one of a kind or is only available for a very limited time draws the shopper to this merchandise. While there is not much empirical research into this dimen-sion of her behavior, retailers such as Pier One Imports, Family Dollar and Costco have recognized this drive and have developed a strategy that they term their "treasure hunt assortment."[50] QVC CEO Michael George summed up shopping at Costco in this way: "You don't go there just for the bargains. You go for the treasure hunt."[51] These two statements neatly describe the Hunter's intentions as well.

Shopper Types: A Final Word

We have identified and discussed five types of shoppers: Ms. Grab and Go, the Lone Browser, Retail Therapy, "Yo, Girlfriend!" and the Hunter. Each shopper type has an agenda when embarking on a shopping trip.

Some like to shop alone, unencumbered by others (including sales people); others seek the social companionship of shopping with friends. Some like to get in and out of a store in a hurry, others like to linger and browse. It is important to remember that these types are not cast in stone and shopping motivations often vary from one shopping trip to another. The following quote eloquently reminds us of this:

> For me, shopping falls into three categories. One is necessity, two is relaxation, and three is social. Necessity shopping is something I usually do alone with a specific goal in mind and it usually takes no more than an hour [Ms. Grab and Go]. Relaxation shopping is also done alone but more as an opportunity for me to walk, think and buy something if it strikes me as pretty. This shopping has no time limit and is done to spend time alone [Lone Browser]. Social shopping is usually done with someone I want to spend time with. It can be a female or male (I have male friends that love to shop) and usually involves food. This shopping trip is about hanging out with someone I like ["Yo, Girlfriend!"] (age 50s).

In this chapter, we reviewed many research studies and explained how the underpinnings of each shopper motivation have been confirmed independently by consumer behavior researchers. For all of these shopper types, other researchers have investigated and reported on dimensions of their behavior. The two primary shopping values that stimulate our shopper types are utilitarian and hedonic. The utilitarian value is most closely linked to Ms. Grab and Go, who strives for efficiency and economy when shopping. Hedonic shopping value, the pleasure dimension, is more complex and its essence can be found in the Lone Browser, "Yo, Girlfriend!" the Hunter, and Retail Therapy.

What we demonstrate in this chapter is that the pleasure derived from shopping is multifaceted and that there are a variety of shopping styles reflecting general attitudes to shopping, positive as seen in the Lone Browser or negative as in Ms. Grab and Go. Other styles are related to mood, as in Retail Therapy; social engagement as in "Yo, Girlfriend!" and, of course, the focused challenge of finding a bargain so evident in the Hunter.

A Note: Why Do Women Love to Browse and Shop?

Long have men complained that women spend hours "shopping" without buying anything. What could motivate women to throw away their time so frivolously? Perhaps as the quote below identifies, women simply gain pleasure from the activity, or if going with friends, shopping provides them with a setting for social interaction. Clearly, shopping and browsing fulfill emotional needs especially when such seemingly (to men) mundane activities are elevated to the status of a "trip." For example, Falk and Campbell (1997) undertook research so that we can understand more about women and browsing while they shop. They tell us:

> It is seen as essential not just because it is the only means of obtaining information about the full range of items available for purchase, but also because it is recognized that it is only through direct exposure to the items for sale that the experience of "desire" which generates "wanting" can occur. However, in addition to this, women speak of the pleasure that can be gained from the activity of shopping whether any purchases are made or not. They refer, for example, to the pleasure to be had in "just looking around," or in "being able to wander and look at things in a way which suggests that a fundamentally aesthetic and expressive gratification is involved. In fact, women are much more likely than men to refer to shopping in terms that imply an enjoyable leisure-time activity in its own right, on a par with tourism for example, as when they speak of a shopping "trip." Consequently women often look forward to going shopping, and in contrast to the men, often embark on a trip without any very specific idea of what they intend to buy.[52]

CHAPTER 6

The Shopping Experience and How to Improve It

In this chapter, we look at several of the elements that create the shopping experience for in-store and online shoppers. In recent decades, retailers have responded to increased competition and developed new formats that are highly engaging for customers, formats that come under the generic term of "experiential retailing." We include a discussion of the concept of experiential retailing as it applies to in-store (bricks and mortar), the mall, and the online shopping experience. We start with a review of some of the research into experiential retailing, including our own studies with comments from our interviewees. From 2003 to 2009, we conducted a cross-cultural and international study where we carried out over 70 in-depth, face-to-face interviews in Australia, the United Kingdom, South Africa, and the United States. We posed several open-ended questions to women about whether they had relationships with retailers (and their salespeople) and what they sought from such relationships. The following section looks at what women want from sales associates and describes a range of customer requirements from the different types of shoppers. The conclusion is that "one size does not fit all" and that retailers need to ensure that staff are well trained to work with their customers.

Experiential Retailing: The Theater of Retail

Experiential retailing is defined as "a strategy that transforms products and services into a total consumption experience, including aspects that are both utilitarian and hedonic."[1] The development of the store as an experience for the customer is now mainstream. The product is no longer the focus; it becomes part of the store atmosphere. Most retailers now seek to build their retail brand and present an environment that customers will seek out as a destination and "linger longer" both online and in-store.

It was the shopping malls of the 1970s that first began the voyage from simply offering retail space in which to display product to offering retailing as an experience. During this decade, many malls introduced food courts and demonstrations, musical performances, and celebratory visits. The hypercompetitive retail environment has encouraged retailers to take a different and broader view of the shopping experience. Retailers have traditionally focused the store environment on highlighting the products, with the retailer and the customer engaging in an economic transaction. The product has been showcased by manufacturers and marketers making it better, cheaper, faster, and available sooner or in a wider range of colors. Advertisers have provided retailers with vast amounts of promotional material that, at times, appears to dominate the store. The challenge for retailers is to change that environment to place more focus on the customer and her experience in the store rather than just the product. Retailers seek to distinguish their stores among the many stores stocking a particular product so that the customer will be attracted to their store.

In experiential retailing, the store becomes the product. The store is not just the site of an efficient transaction. Using the concepts of experiential retailing, the store environment combines the elements of aesthetics, entertainment, education, and escapism. All these elements shift between the static and dynamic mode in the store environment.[2] The static elements are the tangible features of the shop, including the products and store fixtures, fittings, signage, and packaging. These elements are used to create the brand image and experience, communicating messages directly to the customer. Dynamic elements "emphasize human interaction through the customer-staff-store interface."[3] The combination of the static and dynamic elements of the store experience can be seen as a form of theater, with the customer and staff as actors, and the store as the stage.[4] The retail theater allows customers to form their own experience in-store, "taking cues from the static environment of the store in order to produce the dynamic characteristic of the retail experience."[5]

> Shoppers can engage in experiential retailing in a way that transforms an ordinary transaction into an extraordinary engagement with the retailer. The engagement is designed to enhance the experience so

that customers will seek out the store and stay loyal over time. The development of a store experience can involve a significant investment by the retailer and the returns need to be high. These experiences are an economic offering to the customer: "An experience is a distinct economic offering. Today consumers unquestionably desire experiences, and more and more businesses are responding by explicitly designing and promoting them."[6]

Pine and Gilmore (1998) refer to this trend as the "Experience Economy" where the experience created may be the only factor differentiating the store from competitors. With the myriad of options available to consumers and their desire for a more enjoyable experience, the need for higher quality, more experiential, more engaging, and more complex retail environments has significant implications for retailers.[7] There are many cues within the store that will influence, either positively or negatively, the experience that customers will have.[8] Some of the most influential aspects of creating the experience are cues in the store environment and the role of employees:[9] "Stores have distinct environments and marketers understand that the environment of a store is an important part of the shopping experience."[10]

The role that employees play in the retail experience is a crucial factor.[11] Careful planning by sales associates in creating the experience will entail an understanding of these cues and the effects they have on targeted consumers.[12] The marketing scholar, Philip Kotler was one of the first to properly identify atmospherics as a marketing tool for retailers. He defined atmospherics as "the effort to design buying environments to produce specific emotional effects in the buyer that enhance their purchase probability."[13]

Kotler made an important distinction between the intended and the perceived atmosphere. The perceived atmosphere will vary based on consumers' learned responses to colors, noises, sounds and temperatures. The greater the differences between customers, the more varied their perceptions.[14] This has implications for retailers in relation to gender as it is expected their responses to cues and stimuli in the environment will differ.[15] While there has been some research into gender differences in shopping styles,[16] there is still much to learn. What is known is that retailers who know their customers well will be better able to create a more compelling "stage" for the retail experience.

Several research studies found that manipulating atmospheric variables will influence the amount of time spent in-store, willingness to buy, patronage intentions, and perceptions of merchandise value and store image.[17] Recent research links customer's perceptions of sales staff service levels to the merchandise category.[18] This research has shown that customers expect more from the sales staff in a premium store and that the premium store atmosphere will lead to higher patronage expectations. So, the in-store experience has to be congruent with the perceived merchandise image and value; this was experienced by one of our respondents who was purchasing a luxury car. She enjoyed being "pampered" during the experience. The in-store experience is important to women, whether they are purchasing jeans or making a major investment such as buying a car.

The Red Carpet Treatment

For some shopping experiences, receiving exceptional customer service creates a memorable experience for the shopper as well as a strategic advantage for the firm.

> Respondent: I guess the other thing that was really appealing about the Lansing dealer . . . they were very quick in responding and following up and the service was extremely personalized . . . and they treated you really nice. Every time I walked in to the dealer, people greeted me, they asked me if I wanted coffee, so I felt like I really got the red carpet treatment. I mean the bottom line was clearly the price but I was really happy to buy it there because I got such excellent service. Like I said, they gave me the red carpet treatment and it just meant a lot. Because I am paying a lot for a car, and then you do that and get crummy service, well you know, I'd rather take my business somewhere else. Lexus, the dealership there, is just awesome; they really treat people really nice, you go in; they don't make you wait to talk to somebody, somebody is available to talk to pretty much right away, and if you have an appointment they are there at the time that they scheduled

your appointment. They are extremely punctual and their waiting area is very nice, there are magazines, they have a flat panel TV, and it's just very competent, they have coffee and cookies, it's just a very comfortable setting.

Interviewer: How did it make you feel?

Respondent: How did it make me feel . . . pampered I guess, I felt totally pampered. Almost like going to a spa. And you are buying a car, and there are men there and they treat you really nice (age 46).

Experiential retailing goes beyond the simple product focused transaction. The customer has the opportunity to learn about the product or category, to socialize, or to be entertained. For example, in the Niketown store (Chicago), a customer can try on a basketball shoe and try it out on the indoor basketball court; in Williams-Sonoma, they can use a kitchen gadget, not just watch a demonstration; in Sephora, they can take home a sample of perfume, and in some optical stores, they can see how they look with different spectacle frames using in-store video capture. The application of experiential retailing extends beyond big ticket or luxury items and is available in day-to-day shopping. The specialty grocery retailer, Whole Foods, believes that they have created a "Third Place" (see chapter 3). According to A. C. Gallo, co-president of Whole Foods, "We evolved into a 'Third Place.' Outside work and home, for people to hang out, eat, and be with other people."[19]

This understanding that customers need to have a place to be provides Whole Foods with a distinct competitive advantage in the market. Whole Food customers are encouraged to linger and enjoy the store experience. Another supermarket (Wegmans) has embraced experiential retailing in-store, adding tasting, sipping, cooking, and watching to the normal humdrum experience of buying the weekly groceries.

Other stores, like Build-A-Bear Workshop, provide a "hands-on" experience, with the store becoming a playground factory stocked with items the customer can use to create their own bear. All the available materials and trims allow the customer to individualize their bear. The ability for people of all ages to create an object associated with love, loyalty, and fun has led to the success of the Build-A-Bear Workshop business model.

Another novel and compelling experience was developed by Hyundai. They are bringing the car to the customer by installing test drive facilities for their cars in Westfield America malls in California. The in-store experience and experiential retailing is now very well established and customers are seeking similar experiences online.

Experiential Retailing Online

The online format for experiential retailing has taken off quickly and successfully because of the application of new technologies to enhance the customers' experience of the online store. For example, online apparel merchandisers have facilities for a virtual dressing room matched to the customers' sizing and coloring. The female customer enters her measurements and is able to see how a particular garment will fit her. This eliminates many returns and allows the customer to make a more informed decision, particularly when combined with online chat facilities.

Stew Leonards is a supermarket retailer who extends experiential retailing to the online environment by offering a link to "cow cam," live audio links to listen to the farm animals and the ability to download coloring books. The website features picture albums of customers showing their Stew Leonard shopping bags all around the world.[20] Trader Joe's stores take pride in educating their customers with online information about their produce including "TJs Guides for the Culinary Curious." (See http://www.traderjoes.com.)

All these experiences in-store or online are where the products become part of the total experience; they are inputs to the creation of the shopping atmosphere. So, it is clear that contemporary retailing requires the effective implementation of a range of elements contributing to the total shopping experience.

We assert that the key to the in-store experience remains the sales associate and in this next section we describe what our interviewees want from in-store sales staff.

What Women Want in a Relationship
(With Retail Salespeople)

The exchange between salesperson and customer-is the defining moment in a store's existence.[21]

This quote captures the critical nature of the relationship between customers and sales staff. This interaction is part of a range of aspects of the shopping experience that need to be addressed by the retailer in order to be successful. We look at several aspects of the shopping experience sought by women shoppers with a focus on the relationship between customers and sales staff and then discuss strategies to more effectively develop this relationship.

If the exchange between the salesperson and the customer is the defining in-store moment, then it must be coherent with the rest of the store atmosphere. Volumes have been written about establishing a "relationship" with customers as a way to gain competitive advantage, yet most of the discussion focuses on frequency or reward programs rather than on the quality of the interaction between customers and salespeople.[22] We agree with the values of customer relationship management (CRM) assisted by technology, but see a need to continue to improve the in-store experience, where the sale is transacted.

We believe that there is no doubt that the role of the sales associate changed significantly with the introduction of new technology. Yet the focus on CRM has distracted attention from the need for relationship building to occur in-store. For a relationship to exist, some level of human interaction is required. Further, one must recognize that relationships are reciprocal, adaptive, and voluntary. Both parties must have some basic understanding of one another's needs if a relationship is to work. For relationships to deepen, one must invest time and effort. While some retailers invest in "relationship marketing," they may not be focusing on the interpersonal skills necessary to form a relationship with the customer and make it grow. Yet, it is not clear that we understand what the customer wants to experience in this exchange. We now examine what women shoppers seek in a relationship with a retailer (and its salespeople) and discuss what we have found from our research.

We investigated what women customers seek in a relationship with salespeople and whether all customers want the same thing. If not, what differences exist among women customers? A variety of definitions exist for relationship and many are contextual, such as exchange relationships or relationship marketing.[23] We define the store to customer relationship as *a temporary accord or alliance to meet the needs of the customer.*

Only a few studies examined the nature of the relationship between sales associates and retail customers. This topic was approached in different ways, either by classifying sales service problems or identifying success factors in forging sales associate–customer relationships.[24] One team of researchers examined the factors involved in building successful sales relationships. They interviewed sales associates and senior business managers, and conducted in-store customer interviews. They concluded that there are three factors that facilitate the development of long-term customer relationships. The first is a top management–customer orientation, the second is employee–customer orientation, and the third is the patronage of relationship-motivated customers.[25] The study did not examine nor did it reveal any diversity in the types of sales relationships that were sought by customers.

One study of interpersonal influences (e.g., greetings and offers of assistance) revealed that customers had a more favorable attitude toward merchandise and service quality when the sales associates provided social cues such as greetings and assistance with locating goods.[26] While these findings are useful, the diversity of relationships sought by different types of customers is not revealed. Hence, we added to the knowledge of sales associate to customer relationships with our study of women shoppers.

As mentioned, we defined a relationship as an accord or an alliance. For any relationship to survive it must be reciprocal; for example, both parties need to derive a benefit from the alliance, regardless of the amount of time spent on the activity. From our research, we found that retail customers seek different types of relationships with sales associates. The level of relationships our participants sought varied by shopper motivation and the shopping context. For example, no one expected to find sales assistance in discount stores, but when they went shopping for electronics, they did have that expectation.

One finding from our interviews was that some women (with apologies to Greta Garbo) "want to be alone." Many women told us that they wanted to spend their time in the store uninterrupted, apart from an initial greeting from the sales associate. They were seeking time out from their own schedules to browse and have some time alone to see what is new, fresh, or interesting in a store. The Lone Browser and sometimes Retail Therapy shoppers are likely to favor this sort of relationship.[27] She wants a cordial, but distant, relationship with a sales associate that is built on respect and trust, as the following quote illustrates:

> She said, "Oh hi, how you doing? And how's your day going?" And she was just really friendly. And I said . . . great . . . doing great. Well, she goes, "Is there anything specific that you are looking for?" And I said no I'm just browsing, looking for fall clothes. She goes, "Feel free to look around for as long as you want and if you need anything just let me know. I am here to help you." Which I just love, I feel welcomed in a store like that but I don't like a salesperson right at my side just looking over my shoulder to try to help me. I kind of like to be free to browse but if I have questions I like somebody fairly nearby to be able to ask questions (age 46).

Even though she likes to be allowed to look around on her own, The Lone Browser does not want to be ignored, being greeted is very important, as is knowledge that the store staff will available when she needs help:

> I don't want someone following me around right on top of me, but I want to know that if I have a question I can find somebody without having to look too far to find them. It's true though, it's interesting when I think about that because even in stores that are a couple of my favorite stores that I would shop in, if I went in there and was completely ignored by everyone in there, I probably would leave (age 60).

Far from wanting to be alone, we found that many women actively seek stores with associates who can provide her with the knowledge and expertise she seeks. High involvement purchases, from the latest electronic gadget to the selection of knitting patterns and yarns, led one of the interviewees to be loyal to particular stores and to recommend them highly to others. Women like this seek expertise from salespeople. Some are investment shoppers and spend regularly, with quality and understanding of the product high on their agenda. These shoppers seek stores that provide sales associates with expertise. One respondent calls them her "go to people." Alternately, she will actively reject the stores that do not have well trained staff. She enthusiastically talks about the level of service provided in Apple Stores and Williams-Sonoma:

> You're spending a lot of money, so I'm thinking that the people that work there should be able to tell me stuff. They don't know nothing! I hate that. I don't understand. I don't understand that as a concept. Just think how much more stuff you can sell, that the people would be happy with. They would have bought the right thing if they had somebody that understood the stuff. Now, on the flip side of it, I don't have an Apple, but I have an iPod, and they have these little Apple Stores. Those people are well trained in the Apple Stores, and that is a different experience. You know, they got the stuff sitting out, and you can play with it, and ask questions about it like at Williams-Sonoma. You know William-Sonoma? I spend a lot of time in there, too . . . But that's one of my little places that I usually go like once a week, and there is a gentleman in there, I love the fact that the person that's the most knowledgeable person in the cook shop is a man, but he's my go to person (age 50).

Seeking good product knowledge is very important to some shoppers, whereas, for others, the importance of building a relationship with sales staff involves the ability to negotiate the best arrangement and prices possible. We spoke at length with a mature woman who saw it as very important that the relationships she built with sales staff and their managers allowed her to negotiate. She was committed to getting what she wanted, when she wanted it, the pay off for the store being that she spends lots of money on a regular basis. She said,

> I will tell her or him, "Now . . . I really like this article, I really like this dress" or whatever it might happen to be, "but it's way overpriced, and you'll probably be putting it on sale. Would you like to check with the manager and see if he can do that now?" (age 60).

Some women seek a "give and take" relationship with salespeople. The relationships built with these salespeople allow her to go into stores ahead of time to take advantage of good prices. For example, the week before Senior (discount) Day she will approach her favorite salesperson at Macy's and identify the merchandise she wants to purchase. The salesperson will charge the items to her credit card, and later she will go to the store to collect her purchases. Ms. Grab and Go's relationship with the sales staff involves them recognizing her presence, helping her locate the goods she wants, and helping her to proceed rapidly through the point of sale so she can finish the transaction and leave the store quickly. "I shop by myself because I don't like the waiting for people to look at things and I like to get in and out of a store without wasting time" (age 20s).

This type of customer does shop and does spend and tends not to be price sensitive; she just does not want to have to spend a great deal of time doing it. Hence, her relationship with sales staff will be a long and loyal one if the sales staff can give her the prompt service that she wants:

> The service people that will come up to me and help me. I can tell them what I'm looking for, what I need, and they help me out, and I can get in and out as quickly as possible. I'll always go back to a place like that, because, I just, I can't search for things (age 30s).

Some Retail Therapy shoppers will occasionally, but not always, seek social interaction with the salespeople. This type of customer may build relationships with store staff to provide her with social interaction. Although some women do want sales staff to form relationships with them, those relationships do not necessarily have to be with a particular individual:

> I'll definitely go back to the store—it's not a relationship in that whether she's there or not probably will not make a difference as to whether I'm going to shop there. That experience though was very positive and I'll definitely go back, hoping maybe the next salesperson is like that too. But it's not to the point that

the relationship is so that I decide my shopping because of that particular saleswoman (age 46).

We use the results of our research to inform the next sections and to provide suggestions about what retailers can do to more effectively meet the customer service needs of women in the store.

Appropriate Service: Greet Us, but Give Us Space

Most women appreciate being greeted when they enter a store. The greeting acknowledges the salesperson's awareness of their presence and is a welcoming gesture. Two quotes from women at opposite ends of the age spectrum illustrate this point:

> Well it is all right if they [salespeople] say, "well may I help you?" and then if you say no and they say "well fine, if you need anything get a hold of me." Why that's fine, but I don't want them following me around (age 76).

And from the younger woman,

> As far as like sales associates are concerned, all I want is somebody who will greet me, and then if I'm trying to get their attention, that they respond and so I know that they will not be ignoring me (age 26).

We found that most women hate to be followed around while browsing. They want space to look around: "When I'm shopping for clothes, good service is *just don't bother me*, but I don't want to have to look for you when I get ready to ring up."

Another woman said with good humor, "At Victoria's Secret they have so many people and they are right on you—*Back off.*" Sometimes being followed around gives women the impression that they are potential shoplifters: "Give me some space. You feel like they think you're gonna swipe something." It makes them feel uncomfortable. No one likes to feel that they are not trusted.

But they also want salespeople to pay attention and be available when help is needed, especially when the customer is in the dressing room:

> It's also kind of irritating sometimes when you get back in the dressing room, and you need a different size or you'd like to try the other color, and you can't find anybody and you're already half undressed, you know, so you go traipsing out, looking really stupid, well, not naked, but you may have on whatever, and so that gets to be irritating (age 60).

While it is important to give women space to shop, being attentive in discerning when a customer wants and needs assistance is critical. If salespeople are not trained to watch customers' nonverbal behaviors and notice when they are ready for assistance, it can result in an irritated customer or lost business. Two of our interviewees spoke about lost jewelry sales that illustrate this point:

> I did go into a JCPenney once, looking at rings. I must have walked around the counter three or four times with an employee standing right there and not once was I asked if I needed help or wanted to see anything. Needless to say they did not get my business (age 29).

And yet again,

> I walked up to the jewelry counter and there were three salespeople helping this one woman who had an outfit. A woman who was probably about 20 years my senior if that . . . three salespeople helping this person, I waited for 20 minutes. And then I get stubborn and then I said I'm going to continue to wait. And so they came up, finally, one person came over and said, "Can I help you?" And I said I was about to purchase four necklaces and because you made me wait so long I'm taking my business elsewhere (age 32).

If multiple salespeople are available, it does not seem to make sense to focus everyone's attention on one customer. At the very least, if one of the salespeople had acknowledged her presence and given her some indication about when assistance might be forthcoming, the sale might have been saved.

Knowledgeable and Willing Salespeople

When women want sales help, they also want someone who knows something about the merchandise being sold, and they can become angry when the salespeople are not well trained. As one respondent put it, "One of my pet peeves, if you're in a specialty store, and they got somebody in the store who is 12 years old and don't know shit, I hate that!"

Being willing to provide the assistance requested is a key factor in retaining customers. In some cases, when women asked salespeople to check on merchandise, they appeared unwilling to do it.

> Like I used to like Express a lot, but when I came to Michigan State and I went to the Meridian Mall and go into Express, I would say, "Okay, well, do you have any of these sizes in the back?" "No, we don't. All we have is what's out." They always had like 2, 4s and 6s, and I'm like, "Come on, you won't even check," They wouldn't even check. "How do you know you don't have it in the back?" And so, the Express is not my favorite place to go, not here (age 26).

As you can see, even though she had been loyal to Express in her hometown, her experiences in another store tarnished that loyalty. In another example, one young woman felt the frustration of no one wanting to help:

> I was frustrated because the clothes weren't what I was looking for and I felt no sales associate even wanted to help. They would just say, "Ahh . . . I don't know really if we have anything that dressy," or stupid comments like that (age 20).

On the positive side, women love to go to stores where salespeople are knowledgeable and they will visit these stores frequently:

> I like to go there (a local bookstore) because they know where the things are . . . If I say I'm looking for a book on something, they

know, they always know right where it is. It is like amazing to me. So . . . I find them very accommodating (age 56).

Receiving attention from salespeople can make women feel special:

Anyway, the employees at J. Crew knew I was ready to buy a lot of stuff and they waited on me hand and foot. Water, coffee, a tailor, were all at my disposal. [Being] treated in such a fashion made me feel important; not just another shopper (age 18–21).

Trusted Relationship With Salespeople

As we discussed earlier in this chapter, some women seek a trusted relationship with salespeople, or as one of our respondents termed it, her "go-to" people. These women are likely to be Ms. Grab and Go or The Hunter. Once these relationships are established, it can be very lucrative for the retailer and very gratifying for the woman who can rely on this trusted relationship to find the merchandise that fits her needs. These salespeople are proactive and know their customers well: their sizes, their likes, and dislikes. This level of service is most likely to occur in a specialty store or department store setting. High-end stores such as Neiman Marcus or Nordstrom are likely to feature this level of service. We would not expect to see it in Walmart or Target. Here is one of Hunter's illustrative quotes about building this type of relationship:

When we had our Jacobson's store, which is a very upscale store, I knew most of the sales clerks, and they knew what I liked, and they would put things back for me, or as soon as it came on sale or another markdown, they would just put it back, put it on the credit card and call me. And then if I had decided I didn't want it, then I could just say, "No, I changed my mind," and it was no issue, but you build these relationships with the people that wait on you. Now I have one gal at what is now Macy's, and I buy everything from her. If I go to Macy's, which I don't go very often, but if I go Macy's. Camie is the only one that I look for to wait on me (age 60).

Another busy professional woman built a long-term relationship with a personal shopper from Nordstrom. She did not have time to shop for herself and grew to rely on her personal shopper:

> I did have a long-term relationship with an associate at Nordstrom. It was a number of years ago when I was working a job that took up a great deal of my time but paid me extremely well. During that time, I didn't have a lot of time to shop, but needed to dress well so I enlisted the aid of a "personal shopper" at Nordstrom. She was *fabulous*! She quickly got to know what I liked and how I liked things to fit. I could count on her to put together the perfect outfit. We actually had an arrangement that allowed her to send me clothes, sight unseen, and credit my account. During this 5-year relationship I never returned anything and spent thousands of dollars. I did occasionally find the time to go to the store and when I did, shopping with her was something like shopping with a good friend (age 50–60).

Department stores, chains, or independent specialty stores would benefit by identifying the women seeking a trusted relationship and cultivating them. Ms. Grab and Go will be looking for salespeople that save her time and energy. The Hunter will be looking for salespeople who help her find a great bargain or a unique item.

Courteous Behavior at All Times

To our surprise, we heard many stories of outrageously rude behavior during some shopping trips. It seems incredible that we would have to include this section, because it seems so obvious that a salesperson should be respectful and treat customers the way they would want to be treated. One woman told us a story about how salespeople in a small quilt shop criticized her when she asked them to special order a bolt of fabric that was not available in the store.

I saw a fabric I really liked. Trouble was, it was in a quilt displayed on the wall and I could not find it on a bolt. After searching through the entire store, I asked a clerk if she could help me. She went looking for someone to help me and a few minutes later I asked the same question of another clerk. She told me emphatically that there wasn't any more of that material. I asked if it could be ordered. I was willing to buy an entire bolt, and she very rudely told me that it could not be ordered; it wasn't available any more. Disappointed, I looked around a little more and actually heard the clerks talking about me, "who did I think I was, asking them to order fabric" (age not given).

Here is the moral of the story: the quilt shop has lost her patronage, permanently:

I had just about decided that I would not shop there anymore, when on a driving tour around Lake Superior, I found the same fabric in a small quilt store in Minnesota. The clerk who cut it said, "Oh yes, it was very popular." She could hardly keep it on the shelf, she was ordering it all the time. Needless to say, since the big, well-known shop didn't want my money—they will not get it. I prefer to shop elsewhere (age not given).

While it seems evident that women should not be ignored when they walk into the store, we heard accounts of women being ignored because of their age (too young or too old): "When I was a little younger, I had money to buy things and was shopping and a salesperson treated me like a child" (age 21).

Salespeople need to be motivated to do their job. Respondents expressed irritation at salespeople that stood around and talked to one another, ignoring the customers.

Sometimes the wait in the store of trying to get waited on, or if you are trying to find out something, you can't find a clerk half the time, or they are busy talking with each other and that really upsets me (age 70).

It makes sense to try to engage customers in conversation. Those that want interaction will connect and many really appreciate the opportunity to chat. Some of the older women in our sample mentioned that they enjoyed talking to salespeople. These women tended to be Retail Therapy shoppers and used shopping as a way to relax and be entertained or just to relieve boredom. Chatting with customers at the checkout provides a chance to confirm that she has made a wise purchase (reducing the chance of a return). One woman appreciated the fact that one of the cashiers at JoAnn Fabrics knew her name.

> Yeah, she would know my name, yeah. And she always says, "Oh, you got a good bargain." Or, "Boy, that's a nice looking picture or flowers, boy you got a good price on that," or something (age 70).

Worse than being ignored, is experiencing prejudiced behavior from salespeople. Sadly, we also heard about blatant discrimination in some shopping experiences. A respondent recalled an incident from over 30 years ago:

> Respondent: Luxury stores are interesting because, they're interesting for a woman of color because the clerks are sort of assessing you, and when I lived in Miami, it was really interesting. There's a luxury mall called Bal Harbour. We'd go across the bridge to go to this place, and so they've got like Armani . . . and so I went there, and security picked me up.
> Interviewer: What do you mean picked you up?
> Respondent: Picked me up, security.
> Interviewer: Stopped you?
> Respondent: Stopped me. I didn't have any bags. I didn't have anything, but it was . . .
> Interviewer: They stopped you and . . .
> Respondent: They stopped me, and they put me in the security office, and they questioned me . . . at this point in Miami's history, the only people of color who were ever seen in Bal Harbour were people who were cleaning up and stuff, so I was there, and I was shopping, so they were trying to figure out who I was and why I didn't know the rules of the game, and I couldn't possibly be there trying to buy anything "'cause you ain't got that kind of

money," so they made me give them my boss's name, and they
called my boss at home, and he had to vouch for me (age 50).

The above incident happened over 30 years ago, demonstrating that
women remember and recount instances of discrimination in retail for a
very long time. Another African American woman related the following
recent experience when shopping in London:

> My worst shopping experience was when I was in London . . . I
> was in Harrods and the sales clerk would not give me service. I had
> my credit card ready and the item in my hand and [she] would
> not give me any service. I knew then why Oprah had such a bad
> experience (age 21).

Apart from blatant racial discrimination, we heard a number of tales
about women shopping for big ticket items and being patronized by the
salesperson. It is crucial that sales staff treat women as intelligent beings.
We advise that salespeople don't treat women as if they know nothing about
the product, unless they tell you that. Let their questions guide you. Paying
attention and listening to what women say will yield dividends in the form
of loyal customers. One professional woman changed her mind about buying a Nissan because of the way that she was treated at a Nissan dealership:

> I've had an experience at the Nissan dealership where they kind
> of treated me like a dumb female and that was a big turn off for
> me because I consider myself a fairly educated woman and I can
> purchase a car, make a purchasing decision on a car just as well as
> a man. I think if I do enough studying I can understand a car as
> much as a man does . . . At one point I was also looking into an
> Armada . . . but . . . the salesperson I dealt with was such a big turn
> off that I didn't go back there. Turn off; he kind of gave me the feel-
> ing that I was this dumb female, and that really actually turned me
> off from the dealership and ultimately turned me off from the Nis-
> san, that experience (age 46).

This professional woman bought a new and expensive Lexus instead and
continues to enjoy patronizing the Lexus dealership where she is treated

well. Another woman discusses her attitude toward dealing with "big ticket" salespeople:

> I'm definitely more of a techie than my husband is. But, just the way that they talk to me when I'm asking questions. It is all like, oh little girl. It is kind of like when you take your car in, you feel like an idiot, even though I can change my own oil and I can change my tires and stuff like that . . . The reality is, is I spend more money than the guys do, so you better talk to me. But, I'm not necessarily afraid of asking for what I want when I come to those situations, because it is, it is my money. I've worked very hard for it and I will spend it where people treat me well. And so I do find someone who is willing to give me a very honest and comprehensive answer and are very willing to engage me in whatever the product is, then they definitely, that makes for a positive experience. And I'm much more likely to say okay, yeah, it is 20 bucks more than the other store, but I'm willing to pay for it here (age 32).

Earlier in this chapter we spoke about the importance of sales associates to the total in-store experience and how sales associates should be "partners" with their customers. Although some people are naturally inclined to customer service, other sales staff need training and guidelines on work performance and standards. It was depressing for us to read of instances of outright discrimination and rudeness in stores. Such antagonistic behavior will result in significant loss of business as women use their power of recommendation and word of mouth to spread the story of their poor experience in a retail store. To summarize, there appears to be a continuum of relationship levels that women seek with salespeople. At one end is the shopper who wants to be greeted and then left alone; at the other end, the Grab and Go shopper wants immediate and efficient attention from sales people and there are women who are seeking concentrated social interaction with the sales staff.

We conclude that "one size does not fit all" when building relationships between retail salespeople and customers. One common thread was that women want to be greeted and made to feel welcome, which confirms other research findings.[28] Retailers should provide training that will allow salespeople to interpret body language and other nonverbal cues to recognize each type of customer. Recent work[29] indicated that sales performance was improved when sales associates used adaptive selling techniques. We see an opportunity to link adaptive techniques with the findings of our study to pinpoint what occurs when the needs of the customer are identified and responded to correctly. Some women will be very direct (e.g., Ms. Grab and Go): when you ask them if they want help, they will immediately say yes and tell you what they need. The needs of other women are more difficult to discern. For the customer who "wants to be alone," if she says she doesn't want help, she means it. Just give her space to browse, but be attentive if she makes eye contact with you; if she does, then, she probably does want help. Sometimes the best service is simply learning to observe behavior, listening carefully to what is being said, and responding appropriately.

Retailers' Investment in Retail Salespeople

Retail sales staff are now partners with the retailer and the customer in the creation and delivery of a retail experience.[30] They play a major role in the success or failure of the retail store and are increasingly expected to have knowledge of a wide range of products and services. Surprisingly, wholesale and retail trade spends less on training than any other industry, averaging only $179.59 per employee in 2004 versus $1,278.16 per employee in finance, insurance, and real estate.[31] Yet, training can pay off in establishing a brand identity and will assist employees in representing the retail brand.[32] Companies spending an average of $900 per employee per year on training were 57% more profitable than those that spent one third as much.[33] While some retailers make a major investment in sales training, many do not. An informal survey of retail sales associates revealed "associates often exhibited annoying customer service behaviors such as either a lack of or an overabundance of care."[34] Researchers examined the scope and deficiencies in retail sales training and found that only 22% of salespeople received extensive training.[35] Further, retail sales training frequently lacked instruction in selling skills. Seldom do retailers provide training in both product knowledge and customer service.[36] To build customer relationships, retail salespeople need to acquire both product knowledge and an ability to assess customer service requirements. We call on the industry to invest in training sales staff to be knowledgeable about the product and responsive to the needs of customers. The investment in the skills of staff will be rewarded with improved customer loyalty and sales.

CHAPTER 7

Implications and Conclusions

This book has reviewed current understanding and presented research findings of the shopping interests, preferences, and motivations of the single most powerful consumer in the world. As discussed in chapter 1, women are expected to contribute $28 trillion to retail spending by 2014. For the retail industry, an understanding of women, their motivations and preferences for shopping is critical. It is women who, at this stage in retail history, determine whether a retail business survives, thrives, or fails.

In this concluding chapter, we review and summarize the findings from our many interviews with American women. We focus on the underlying motivations for shopping and provide a section on practical advice for the retail industry. This section will be of particular relevance to retailers, marketers, advertisers, and promotion staff, suppliers, and mall managers.

The chapter begins with a profile of the contemporary American woman from the baby boomer to Generation Y. The history of American women follows that of the growing nation and the retail industry has changed and developed as the status of women has changed. Included in this section is a review of intergenerational shopping and skills transfer and the shopper typology. The motivations for shopping are highlighted as we look at the utilitarian and hedonic shopper. Wishes such as independence, creativity, social interaction and the seeking of retail therapy are discussed.

The last section of this chapter provides suggestions and recommendations for members of the retail industry. Topics include the following:

- shopper marketing
- appealing to the various types of shopper

- suggestions for store design
- visual merchandising and experiential retailing
- store policies and procedures
- acknowledging intergenerational shopping

The Contemporary American Woman

It was noted that retailing changed throughout contemporary history as the status of women changed. There is every reason to believe that this will continue and retailers need to be alert to shifts in demographics. One major opportunity for retailers in the next 20 years is the female baby boomer segment. These women, who are beginning to retire, are healthier and wealthier than any other cohort of women in human history. This group of women can look forward to several decades of retirement and will be looking for retailers who can make their lives safer and happier. They will be seeking comfortable stores with access for those with limited mobility. Once in a store they will want room to move, low levels of noise so they can hear a full range of sound with their declining hearing, and signage that is large enough to see. Most of all, they will look to be acknowledged as an individual rather than ignored as often happens to older women. At the moment, this group is seriously underserviced:

> It's someone's 50th birthday every 8 seconds in the U.S., but retailers are still obsessively focused on young people. A study by Credit Suisse First Boston, for example, found that in the U.S. there are 7,700 clothing chains selling to the teen market (with a theoretical sales of U.S. $5.8m per store) but only 1,800 (with theoretical sales of U.S. $19.2m per store) targeting baby boomers. As populations age, more people will want to spend more time at home and they will want to make their lives as comfortable as possible. The implications of this demographic shift include everything from a boom in gardening to employing seniors (B&Q) and designing food packaging that people with old hands and poor eyesight can actually open.[1]

The other segment of women presenting opportunities for the retail industry is Generation Y, those born between 1977 and 1994 (now age

16–33). Members of Generation Y are also called the "Millenials." The size of this demographic segment is larger than the baby boomers, estimated to be about 82 million (vs. 78 million baby boomers).[2] This generation is different from baby boomers and Generation X in that it is more racially diverse, with 38% classified as non-White versus 27% of baby boomers.[3] They are tech savvy, having grown up with the Internet. They shop more frequently than previous generations and are very individualistic.[4]

> Gender issues also frame important distinctions about the cohort. Girls and young women are encouraged and expected to have careers. Marriage no longer represents the ultimate goal for many Gen Yers . . . In addition, women—who have traditionally driven purchasing decisions in many categories—are continuing to make progress in business, politics, and other areas of American life. As a result, they have less time for shopping and might be expected to value convenience more highly than in the past.[5]

Retailers and mall managers will need to carefully plan their retail and merchandise mix to satisfy the sometimes competing lifestyles of baby boomers and Generation Y women. For example, the family structure of this generation is not likely to parallel the nuclear family of the baby boomers. Rather, Generation Y is marrying later, bearing children at an older age, and having fewer children than their baby boomer parents. To address these differences, a well known commercial real estate firm suggests the following:

- developing store layouts to appeal to task oriented shoppers
- offering multichannel shopping opportunities to convenience driven shoppers
- developing effective multicultural marketing.[6]

Consumption is a complex issue that crosses all parts of society and as the role of women changes so will the demands on retailers. Shopping, as defined by our interviewees, is a feminized and fun activity. Shopping obviously has many other purposes that engage women differently. There is a need for further research into the role and needs of women in the marketplace so the industry can continue to provide women with an interesting, efficient, and fun experience when they shop. Areas of research that may be of interest to retailers and marketers are the extent to which women engage in "self-gifting," or making purchases that are a reward or a present to themselves to mark some particular, very personal achievement. Self-gifting is a specific example of the general category of going shopping to change moods. Women told us that they will go shopping as a form of time out to renew their spirits or to recover from an unpleasant emotion or experience.

There are a few high priority research areas that relate to the format and style of "Third Places" for women. The mall is a key Third Place in the community despite its private ownership and control of access. There is evidence that mall patronage is on the decline, with slower sales figures as a possible consequence. This decline may result from a variety of factors including the competition from the service economy such as gyms, sporting, and health clubs. It may also be in response to a failure of mall owners and designers to respond to the changing needs of women. Women's increased participation in the workforce at senior levels, increased discretionary income and time pressures, and changes in the global economy may all be contributing to a move away from malls to smaller precincts or home-based shopping. Women may be rejecting malls in a way similar to their rejection of down town shopping in the 20th century. When women went into town to shop, they were greeted by huge department stores with opulent merchandise displays, intensive service, and facilities for their use. The department store provided reading rooms, lounges, health and beauty services, and cultural activities including exhibitions and shows. The contemporary mall, while providing a wide range of stores, does not provide that level of personal facilities for women. Today, the gym may be competing with the mall as the "Third Place" for many women.

Today's women are better educated, often with their own financial and decision-making power and a disposable income to match. Many women are employed full time away from the home; they are having fewer children and marrying later (if at all). Women are key influencers on the retail industry; their powers of recommendation are extensive and they know how to use that power and are not afraid to do so. Viral marketing, the approach to get people talking about a product or service, has sat naturally in a woman's repertoire for a very long time.

The status of women in society has changed dramatically in the last century and the retail industry has had to change in response to the changes in women's lives. For example, when women joined the workforce in great numbers, stores began to offer extended opening hours and provide quick meal options for working mothers. Now, with increased time pressures there are many facilities to make life easier such as prepared meals, frozen meals, and carry out food stores everywhere, all serving people with very busy life styles.

In this book we have attempted to provide the reader with an appreciation of the historical development of the retail industry and how it and the status of women have changed over the last few centuries. This background enables the reader to better understand why particular retail formats such as department stores, boutiques, and the various mall formats, such as lifestyle malls exist; why we have extended trading hours, and why malls exist in the suburbs; why some stores can provide low levels of service and while others need to provide intense customer service.

The reader can now appreciate why it is that women can go shopping for hours, have a great time, and come home without purchasing anything. And most importantly, the reader should have several ideas on how to ensure that this customer has their store at "top of mind awareness" every time she wants to browse, so that when she is ready to spend, she will immediately head to your store. Retailers and mall developers need to provide an experience for a woman that makes the shopping trip part of rest and recreation, not just a chore. As the early department stores demonstrated, shopping could be a social event, an exciting event, an event that is pleasurable and memorable.

Mothers transfer financial, aesthetic, decision making, and budgeting skills to their daughters as part of teaching them the craft of shopping. This process of "consumer socialization" is particularly relevant to marketers, advertising campaign developers, mall managers, and retailers seeking to understand their customers. The daughter may or may not accept what her mother is saying, but she does not forget the rules and attitudes that mom had. One of our interviewees told us that "she shops with her mom (now deceased) on her shoulder." In the adult shopper, the experiences of the young child and the influences of the mom remain.

In this book we have focused on the underlying motivations for women and shopping. These themes include the need for power and independence, creativity and self-identity, and meeting emotional needs. Shopping, as defined by our interviewees, is rarely just a functional necessity for women. We identified five main shopper types, with the first distinction being women who do not enjoy shopping and tend to have high utilitarian motivations (Ms. Grab and Go). The remaining four categories, the Lone Browser, "Yo, Girlfriend!", the Hunter, and those seeking Retail Therapy are motivated by pleasure—the hedonic motivation.

The Utilitarian Shopper

Many marketers and retailers may tend to ignore Ms Grab and Go as she is not an enthusiastic shopper. This is a mistake. Shoppers with high utilitarian motivations have higher store repatronage intentions and have higher loyalty than those who shop for pleasure (hedonic shoppers).[7] Ms. Grab and Go will be a very loyal customer of stores that meet her need for speed and efficiency of service; Ms Grab and Go may not enjoy shopping but she does spend and she is not price sensitive, because she does not want to take the time to look around.

Women who shop for pleasure have different needs in a store than utilitarian shoppers. In general, they are happier when they can browse, either alone or with friends. And the Lone Browser will use her power of recommendation and tell her friends about a good store.[8] When women go shopping to make themselves feel better, they are in search of Retail Therapy. This woman is believed to be either engaging in "compensatory consumption," to, for example, fill a void in her life, or engage in what is called "mood alleviative consumption." She will, for example, go shopping to relieve a bad mood.[9]

The Hedonic Shopper

The chapter on the typology of shoppers presents research findings related to Retail Therapy, including seven reasons why women engage in Retail Therapy. The following are the seven reasons:

- positive distraction
- escape
- indulgence

- elevation of self esteem
- activation
- sense of control
- social connection

The women we spoke with did shop to escape, as one did when she was angry at her husband; positive distraction was described by one woman who shopped to unwind; another mentioned shopping as an indulgence; and elevation of self-esteem and was depicted by women who felt better when they put on new clothes. Interestingly, none of our respondents tended to seek Retail Therapy as a way to connect socially:

> When I'm stressed out I go shopping, just having something new, a new product. It has some kind of meaning, makes you feel good in a way. Perhaps because you look good you feel good, so a new pair of pants or shoes will make me feel confident (age 20).

It is politically incorrect these days to associate the acquisition of things with feeling good. That association is often viewed as shallow materialism. However, acquiring things does make us feel good (if even only for a little while). Sarah and Sharon both felt good from going shopping. Sarah openly stated that she needed to shop—which perhaps is taking things too far. Nevertheless, buying things, or just browsing does provide a release for women shoppers, and is often connected to the need to feel powerful or independent in some aspect of their lives, or as a reward for hard efforts at the workplace or at home.

Women also shop to get away from obligations and have some time for themselves. For example, shopping can provide women with a release from family obligations. Women often refer to shopping alone or with friends as "their time." Janine is a classic example of someone who seeks escape through shopping:

> I tend to shop Friday afternoon with a girlfriend, so that's really nice because it's our time. We look at things we want to look at, whereas if I go with my family I have to look at what the kids want to look at, what my husband wants to see and then you've got to go everywhere. It's nice spending time with them too, but it's certainly not my time (age 39).

Women shop to gain a release—release from obligation, release from negative experiences, and a release from life's difficulties. Behind the jokes about Retail Therapy, there is a very real motivation to seeking therapeutic release from shopping. In times past, shopping was often women's first experience at being treated as an equal in a man's world. Such motivations continue to this day. Women seek to display their financial independence through shopping, and as a result seek feelings of being in control and empowered while they shop. This often explains why women respond so strongly to poor service and why they continue to patronize stores that treat them well (i.e., with the respect they feel they deserve). Independence can also be expressed through an individual identity.

The Creative Homemaker

People shop for things that reflect their real or desired ideal self. For many of the women we interviewed, shopping was part of a creative act. Women would shop for items that would help reflect their identity to others, exemplified in the market mavens.

Women seek creative expression in a variety of settings including interior design and decoration. The nesting behavior of the last few years has led to a rapid increase in home decorating as an activity for creative self expression. As Gabriel and Lang stated,

> Western consumers spend enormous amounts of time decorating their homes, choosing their clothes, food, and other goods, planning their holidays, forever mixing ingredients, as if they were trying not merely to create works of art but to discover a uniquely individual style. To do so, commodities must appear forgetful of being use-values, and must appear exclusively as objects of pure taste.[10]

Today these designs are seen as impermanent, with consumers changing rooms, or home designs in the same way, and as frequently as they would change a season's style of fashions. For women in particular, the home's appearance has become a major preoccupation, and due to rising incomes, spending on the home has become a top priority for women. Since the 1990s, spending on home renovation has been increasing.

Decorating and gardening are the fastest growing product categories for Michael's and Home Depot. This desire to express one's creativity also motivated many of our women to search for what they called "real things" or "treasures."

Shopping is about expressing oneself and seeking to be creative. Women search for goods that express their identities through creative acts. This may be through the purchase of finished products that express individual identities (such as luxury brand names or boutique products), or products with historical value. Shopping also plays an important social role for women.

Social Interaction

Shopping gives women an opportunity to interact with others and is one of its positive aspects, as acknowledged in the following quote:

> Retailing provides us with another "good" that is rare or absent from the rest of our lives: places to gather enjoyably with other people. Look at, for instance, Starbucks and Borders bookstores; if we don't have gazebos on town greens, we do have lounge chairs in stores like these.[11]

While some women may use shopping as a way of proving their independence and power, for others it serves a much deeper purpose of fulfilling social needs.

People need social interaction. Consumers often desire to return to times past because they are perceived as being simpler, safer, and better than the present. Currently, many consumers are placing greater emphasis on close personal relationships with businesses and employees out of a desire for social interaction. Some consumers continue to want more direct relationships with providers and to feel that they are dealing with a human being. In retail, this has led to a rise in boutique stores, which are successful because they embrace highly personalized operations, and offer familiarity and quality merchandise. As an antidote to the sense of isolation and insecurity that many people feel, women want to be acknowledged in the retail setting. Politeness is now seen as important, expected, and something that sets a business apart.

Shopper Marketing and Women

There is evidence that many women spend considerable effort researching and planning their shopping trips. For the "Yo, Girlfriend!" shopper, the planning of a shopping trip can start up to a year ahead. Some women plan out the route for their expedition; others read sales ads and clip (or download) coupons, these activities indicate that shopping is a task worthy of preparation. The challenge for retailers is to embrace some of the emerging knowledge about shopper marketing that considers the entire shopping process, from the preshopping phase into the store or mall, to point of purchase, and in-store promotion, followed by after sales care and attention. Currently, smart phone applications offered by retailers (e.g., notification about new merchandise and personalized discounts) address the preshopping phase and attempt to draw customers into the store. Many retailers now gather information about the in-store shopping experience via a sales receipt web link to an online survey, but other opportunities exist to improve the postpurchase process, especially for big ticket items.

In this next section, we offer strategies and tactics about how to attract and retain women shoppers. Retailers, marketers, and mall managers can select those that strategically fit their firm.

How to Appeal to the Shopper Types

Ms. Grab and Go is likely to seek help from salespeople. Training sales people to pay attention to women who enter the store and appear to be "on a mission" will pay dividends. She wants someone to help her find the merchandise she is looking for and make her shopping trip as short as possible. A Ms. Grab and Go is a likely customer for a personal shopper. However, not all stores provide that type of service. If your store is a discount store, self-service is expected; you can still meet Ms. Grab and Go's needs by providing an efficient store layout (e.g., grid vs. racetrack) with clearly delineated departments and uncomplicated way finding, such as easy to read signage. Astute use of technology, such as self-checkout, express checkouts, in-store kiosks to locate merchandise, and price check scanners can contribute to a more efficient shopping experience. And store greeters who are knowledgeable on store layout are a real bonus for

Ms Grab and Go. If she doesn't know where to find something she will go straight to the store greeter.

Advertising promotions of new merchandise will bring the Lone Browser to the store. Once there, it is important that sales people greet her, offer assistance, and then back off. If she needs sales assistance, she will ask for it. She likes to look around at her leisure; she will pick up merchandise, examine it, and may or may not purchase it. She will be annoyed at salespeople who "nip at her heels" with a running commentary on merchandise benefits; in fact, such behavior from salespeople may motivate her to leave the store. Enticing displays of new or innovative merchandise will attract her. In some venues (e.g., book stores), a place to sit and enjoy a beverage will also be inviting to her and encourage her to linger. Rest facilities are important to the Lone Browser as she will often spend many hours browsing.

Marketing to the Retail Therapy shopper might involve several strategies. For those who shop because they are bored or lonely, encourage salespeople to be friendly and try to engage this shopper in conversation as she enters the store. Within a few seconds, the salesperson should be able to assess whether she wants to chat or not. To entertain bored shoppers, in-store or mall-wide events will attract this shopper. This is where creating a unique retail experience can pay off. We discussed examples of successful experiential strategies in chapter 6. The Retail Therapy shopper may be sad, dejected, bored, lonely or angry; or she may want to celebrate an achievement, a recovery, or her own birthday. On these occasions, she may be looking for self-gifts (e.g., fragrances, chocolate, jewelry). To the extent possible, highlight the "feel good" qualities of such merchandise. If your firm offers spa or health and beauty services, this is the opportune time to appeal to the Retail Therapy shopper who wants to feel better.

Retailers and mall managers have a unique opportunity to market to the "Yo, Girlfriend!" Programs that invite groups of women to shop your mall (or store) will be attractive to this group. Offering special discounts, demonstrations, or an opportunity to see new merchandise (e.g., trunk shows) can draw groups of women in. Specialty stores might consider hosting private parties of women to shop while closing the store to the general public. Some larger specialty department stores, like Neiman Marcus, frequently have private shopping events for their best customers. When feasible, offering seating or a place to store bags will make waiting for others in the group to finish shopping more pleasant. Big malls should consider making arrangements for joint promotions with local hotels and motels to encourage groups to stay overnight in the location.

The way to attract the Hunter into your store is to put out a rack of merchandise with a "Sale" sign on it, but for many women in this group, the value has to be there. Appealing to the Hunter requires either a well-honed pricing strategy or a willingness to negotiate on price. The other strategy is to offer unique merchandise, such that the Hunter knows she will not find comparable merchandise elsewhere. If your firm is the price leader, then be sure to highlight this in your promotional strategies. Inform the Hunter that she will not find better prices elsewhere. This can be communicated via traditional media, social media, or e-mail. Kohl's, Pier One Imports, and Williams-Sonoma continuously communicate special deals for their customers via e-mail. If you are a discounter, you can still appeal to the Hunter's quest for one of a kind merchandise by implementing a "treasure hunt" strategy similar to that of Costco, where you offer a few hard to find items at competitive prices. You want to encourage the Hunter to share her "finds" with others, perhaps by persuading her to post her successes on Facebook, or the Haul.

Store Design, Visual Merchandising, and Experiential Retailing

Creative and attractive merchandise displays draw customers in. A retailer that is unfamiliar to a potential customer has about 10 to 30 seconds to help her make up her mind about whether to enter a store and to stay once she enters. The following quote makes this point:

> If there is a cute jacket in the window I might go and check it out . . . If there is that one thing that catches my eye and I see it, I might go in . . . Often times, whatever is right out front. I can usually tell if I'm gonna be interested in the store. I can walk in a store, and in 30 seconds I know whether I'm gonna find anything in there or not that I want, I would 90% of the time, and it's that first impact (age 46).

While it may seem intuitive, it is important to create a store layout that invites browsing. Paco Underhill, an urban geographer, articulates a reaction to a crowded shopping environment that he calls the "butt brush theory." After reviewing thousands of hours of tapes of people shopping, he observed that women who are browsing are much less likely to buy merchandise that she is looking at if she is brushed from behind while she is examining it. She will simply put the merchandise down and walk away. "Butt brush" is likely to occur in crowded stores or stores with particularly narrow aisles that leave little room for people to pass one another.[12]

While a crowded shopping environment can create a feeling of excitement and urgency, it is also a turn off to most of our participants, regardless of age. In fact, most of the stories about "worst" shopping experiences include a reference to crowded stores. We are aware that retailers cannot control when people shop and crowded stores are part of the territory. However, crowded shopping environments can be mitigated by paying careful attention to store layout. Provide plenty of room between display racks, and, when feasible, provide wide aisles (for a grocery store, that means enough room for two carts to pass through easily) so that women can browse unimpeded.

Return Policies

Return policies are an important element of a retailer's service portfolio. With an estimated $3.8 billion in fraudulent returns during the holiday season alone,[13] these policies have become stricter and less favorable to the customer. While some of our participants don't like the trend toward more restrictive returns, they understand why it is happening and try to adjust. However, some policies have become so restrictive, that they are a turn off for even loyal customers. For some women, not being able to return merchandise can be a "deal breaker" for a purchase. If she can't return it, she won't buy it. Make your return policies fair and straightforward and your business will reap dividends in store loyalty. Kohl's Department store is an example of a retailer that does this well. Kohl's has developed a hassle free return policy that matches the circumstances of the purchase (online, in-store). Customers can return merchandise even if there is no receipt. Treating customers respectfully when they make returns is critical to future business. Here is one funny and sad anecdote about a failed customer return experience:

> Went to return something to Abercrombie and Fitch and the manager kept smelling it and didn't want to take it back because he thought it smelt like "it was laundered." Tags were on and I had the receipts. Other manager got involved and let me return the items and I was purchasing something else, but have never returned to any Abercrombie store again and never will. Yes, I did call customer service to register a complaint. Never received any reply back (age 49).

Acknowledge Intergenerational Shopping

In many ways, shopping has become a community activity, where women of all ages get together at the mall to meet, have coffee, browse, chat, and shop. Women will gather in mother/daughter or grandmother/mother/daughter groups for a day out, or browse on their own as part of time out, or looking for inspiration. An aspect of women and shopping highlighted in this book is the strength and longevity of the familial ties between mothers/daughters/grandmothers/aunts shopping together. The process of "consumer socialization" has identified the intergenerational influences in learning about shopping. Skills transferred from mother to daughter can include understanding weights and measures, percentages, discounts, and markdowns as well the quality of merchandise in clothing and footwear, or the freshness of fruit and vegetable offers. All these skills go to create an understanding of "value" for money. Our research highlighted the power of the mother/daughter shopping relationship and retailers and marketers can harness some of that power. For example, it is common to see mothers and daughters shopping with a baby in a stroller. When these three generations shop together, they need wider aisles, car parking with room to bring out the stroller, and clean and accessible rest and family rooms.

Other women shared their memories related to the ritual nature of shopping with their mothers and other female relatives. The security and comfort of these regular events was evident and retailers and marketers can build on that security with promotions and staff who recognize the importance of intergenerational shopping. Stores that welcome these intergenerational shoppers are laying the foundation for the future loyalty of the next generation.

More subtly, there is the opportunity to engage with aspects of time poverty and nostalgia when promoting stores and malls. Many of our interviewees spoke fondly of shopping events that occurred many generations ago and appeals to that nostalgia may be attractive to many women.

The key to shopper marketing to women is accepting that one size does not fit all and to educate sales associates so that they have the skills to be able to correctly read the nonverbal or verbal signals of their customers and respond appropriately. The process of shopping is a partnership between the retailer and the customer revolving around the transaction. The challenge is for the retailer to see the store as a place where partnerships can exist. As we have demonstrated, women go shopping for many reasons that have nothing to do with purchasing. It is difficult for retailers to get the mix correct so that the shopping trip is enhanced by a purchase. The partnership works when the customer makes a purchase because the retailer has presented the "right" merchandise well, and the partnership works when store policies are appropriate and fair to the store, the supplier, and the customer. The partnership is about providing a clean, well lit store that, in the case of boutiques, makes it very easy for the customer to try on apparel. The partnership is about polite, knowledgeable staff with the emotional intelligence to try to understand what the customer is seeking and do what is possible to solve the problem for her. The partnership is about the customer being loyal to the store, providing excellent word of mouth recommendations, and treating sales associates with respect.

A Final Word

And of course, there is the "elephant in the room"—men and shopping. Traditionally, men have been the stay at home partner, the bag carrier, and Mr. Whine and Wait. The young men in Generation Y are far more likely to enjoy shopping than their fathers did. These young men are also brand aware and will participate in lengthy shopping trips with their friends. This shift in how men perceive shopping is likely to continue and will provide retailers with access to a huge section of the population. What is not known is what these men will want from retail and how it will differ from the varied needs of women.

For now, in this book, we have demonstrated the importance of the female consumer to the retail industry and that there is no "one size fits all." Retailers can provide a range of strategies to ensure that their offer is attractive to women shoppers and allows them to establish long-term successful partnerships with their customers. The history of retail is embedded in the history of women, and retailers need to pay close scrutiny to how women's lives are changing, particularly in relation to the need for a "Third Place." Finally, we salute all those women we met who generously shared their thoughts and feelings with us.

Notes

Chapter 1

1. Voigt (2009).
2. Shop. In *Merriam-Webster's online dictionary* (2003). http://www.merriam-webster.com/dictionary/shop. (7 Dec. 2010).
3. Hirschman and Holbrook (1982), p. 92.
4. Schroeder (2003).
5. Kershaw (2003); Lambert (2003).
6. Underhill (2000).
7. Barletta (2003); Popcorn and Marigold (2000).
8. Barletta (2003); Popcorn and Marigold (2000); Underhill (2000).
9. Barletta (2003).
10. Popcorn and Marigold (2000), p. 9.
11. Barletta (2003); Rowe (2003).
12. Cameron (2003); Lambert (2003); Protyniak (2003).
13. Tom Peters in Barletta (2003), p. ix.
14. Underhill (2000).
15. Underhill (2000).
16. U.S. National Center for Health Statistics (2009).
17. Bristor and Fischer (1993).
18. Costa (1994).
19. Barletta (2003); Rowe (2003).
20. Fischer and Arnold (1990).
21. Costa (1994); Fisher and Dubé (2003).
22. Bristor and Fischer (1993), p. 519.
23. Costa (1994).
24. Barletta (2003).
25. Hine (2002).
26. Barletta (2003).
27. Otnes and McGrath (2001).
28. Campbell (1997).
29. Otnes and McGrath (2001), p. 147.
30. Otnes and McGrath (2001).
31. Otnes and McGrath (2001).
32. Hine (2002); Underhill (2000).

33. Sherman, Schiffman, and Mathur (2001).
34. Sherman, Schiffman, and Mathur (2001).
35. Moutinho, Davies, and Curry (1996).
36. Moutinho, Davies, and Curry (1996).
37. Underhill (2000).
38. Underhill (2000).
39. d'Astous (2000); Dholakia (1999); Goff, Bellenger, and Stojack (1994); McGrath (1998); Myers-Levy (1989); Shao, Baker, and Wagner (2004); Tingley and Robert (2000).
40. Baker, Levy, and Grewal (1992); Fischer, Gainer, and Bristor (1997).
41. d'Astous (2000); Fischer, Gainer, and Bristor (1998).
42. McGrath (1998).
43. Fischer, Gainer, and Bristor (1997); Shao, Baker, and Wagner (2004).
44. Tingley and Robert (2000).
45. Nelms (n.d.).
46. Barletta (2003); Popcorn and Marigold (2000); Underhill (2000).

Chapter 2

1. Nystrom (1930).
2. Savitt (1989), p. 345.
3. Savitt (1989), p. 345.
4. Harrison (1975).
5. Savitt (1989), p. 347.
6. Savitt (1989), p. 347.
7. Harrison (1975), p. 114.
8. Smith (2008).
9. Kleinberg (1999).
10. Harrison (1975), p. 111.
11. Benson (1986).
12. Savitt (1989).
13. Burns and Rayman (1995), p. 168.
14. Kleinberg (1999).
15. Kleinberg (1999).
16. Kleinberg (1999).
17. May (2000).
18. Mettler (2005).
19. May (2000).
20. Kleinberg (1999), p. 241.
21. Anonymous (2002a).
22. Anonymous (2002a).
23. Anonymous (2002a).

24. Anonymous (2002b).
25. Anonymous (2002b).
26. Anonymous (2002b).
27. Anonymous (2002c).
28. Anonymous (2002c).
29. Muhlebach (2003).
30. Muhlebach (2003), p. 36.
31. U.S. Census Bureau (2008a).

Chapter 3

1. Gorz (1989), pp. 30–31.
2. Rappaport (2000), p. 162.
3. Rappaport (2000), p. 143.
4. Rappaport (2000), p. 166.
5. Zola (1883), p. 128.
6. Feinberg and Meoli (1991).
7. Muhlebach (2003).
8. Oldenburg (2000).
9. Feinberg, Sheffler, Meoli, and Rummel (1989); Green (1998).
10. Bloch, Ridgeway, and Dawson (1994).
11. Sandikci and Holt (1998).

Chapter 4

1. Ward, Wackman, and Wartella (1977).
2. Ward (1974).
3. Popcorn and Marigold (2000).
4. Douglas (1994); Thompson (1996).
5. Minahan and Beverland (2005).
6. Neeley and Coffey (2007).
7. Darian (1998); Rust (1993).
8. Belch, Belch, and Ceresino (1985); Martin (2009); Rust (1993).
9. Darian (1988).
10. Meyer and Anderson (2000).
11. Meyer and Anderson (2000).
12. Martin (2009).
13. Martin (2009).
14. Francis and Burns (1992).
15. Viswanathan, Childers, and Moore (2000).
16. Haytko and Baker (2004), p. 81.

17. Bamossy (1982), p. 38.
18. Lowndes and Moore (1975).
19. Schindler, Lala, and Grussenmeyer-Corcoran (2008).
20. Meyer and Anderson (2000).
21. Green (1998), p. 172.
22. Ward, Wackman, and Wartella (1977).
23. Lachance and Choquette-Bernier (2004); Neeley (2005).
24. Moore, Wilkie, and Alder (2001).
25. Chiaro (2010).
26. Thompson (1996).
27. Kiecker and Hartman (1993).
28. Glass, Bengston, and Dunham (1986).
29. Sorce, Loomis, and Tyler (1989).
30. Gavish, Shoham, and Ruvio (2008).

Chapter 5

1. Babin, Darden, and Griffin (1994); Jones, Reynolds, and Arnold (2006).
2. Jones, Reynolds, and Arnold (2006).
3. Babin, Darden, and Griffin (1994).
4. Babin, Darden, and Griffin (1994).
5. Eroglu and Harrell (1986).
6. Jones, Reynolds, and Arnold (2006).
7. Huddleston, Whipple, and Cho (2010).
8. Jones, Reynolds, and Arnold (2006).
9. Jones, Reynolds, and Arnold (2006); Huddleston, Whipple, and Cho (2010).
10. Babin, Darden, and Griffin (1994), p. 646.
11. Babin, Darden, and Griffin (1994).
12. Cox, Cox, and Anderson (2005).
13. Arnold and Reynolds (2003).
14. Jones, Reynolds, and Arnold (2006).
15. Huddleston, Whipple, and Cho (2010).
16. Jones, Reynolds, and Arnold (2006).
17. Jones, Reynolds, and Arnold (2006).
18. Babin, Darden, and Griffin (1994); Kang (2009).
19. Woodruffe-Burton (1998).
20. Kang (2009).
21. Kang (2009).
22. Woodruffe (1997).
23. Woodruffe (1997).
24. Cox, Cox, and Anderson (2005).
25. Church and Thomas (2006); Graham, Graham, and MacClean (1991).

26. Pettigrew (2007).
27. Kim, Kim, and Kang (2003).
28. Kim, Kim, and Kang (2003).
29. Church and Thomas (2006).
30. Kacen and Friese (1999).
31. Kacen (1998).
32. Woodruffe (1997).
33. Kacen and Friese (1999).
34. Kang (2009).
35. Tauber (1995).
36. Cardoso and Pinto (2010).
37. Borges, Chebat, Babin (2010).
38. Borges, Chebat, Babin (2010).
39. Luo (2005).
40. Feick and Price (1987).
41. Feick and Price (1987).
42. Walsh, Gwinner, and Swanson (2004).
43. Cox, Cox, and Anderson (2005).
44. Babin, Darden, and Griffin (1994).
45. Arnold and Reynolds (2003).
46. Schindler (1989).
47. Tauber (1995).
48. Lai and Aritejo (2009).
49. Meltzer (2010).
50. SanFilippo (2005).
51. McGregor (2008).
52. Falk and Campbell (1997), p. 170.

Chapter 6

1. Kim, Sullivan, and Forney (2007), p. 3.
2. Csikszentmihalyi (1997); Pine and Gilmore (1999).
3. Healy, Beverland, Oppewal, and Sands (2007).
4. Baron, Harris, and Harris (2001).
5. Baron, Harris, and Harris (2001), p. 755.
6. Pine and Gilmore (1999), p. 97.
7. Kozinets et al. (2002).
8. Pine and Gilmore (1999).
9. Schmitt (1999); Baron, Harris, and Harris (2001).
10. Sharma and Stafford (2000), p. 183.
11. Baron, Harris, and Harris (2001).
12. Pine and Gilmore (1999).

13. Kotler (1973/74), p. 50.

14. Kotler (1973/74).

15. d'Astous (2000); Meyers-Levy (1989); Meyers-Levy and Sternthal (1991).

16. Minahan and Beverland (2005).

17. Baker, Levy, and Grewal (1992); Baker, Parasuraman, Grewal, and Voss (2002); Ward, Bitner, and Barnes (1992).

18. Mitchell, Oppewal, and Beverland (2009).

19. Puente (2006), p. 01D.

20. Leonard, 2010.

21. Hu and Jasper (2006), p. 29.

22. Landry, Arnold, and Arndt (2005).

23. Beatty, Mayer, Coleman, Reynolds, and Lee (1996), p. 223.

24. Dotson and Patton (1992).

25. Beatty et al. (1996).

26. Hu and Jasper (2006).

27. Minahan and Beverland (2005).

28. Dotson and Patton (1993).

29. Franke and Park (2006).

30. Weitz and Bradford (1999).

31. Rhode (2006).

32. Brown (2002).

33. Cole-Gomolski (1998).

34. Nagle (2002), p. 7.

35. Pettijohn and Pettijohn (1994).

36. Nagle (2002).

Chapter 7

1. Anonymous (2010d).

2. Miller (2009).

3. Maloney (2002), p. 3.

4. Maloney (2002); Miller (2009).

5. Maloney (2002), p. 5.

6. Maloney (2005).

7. Jones, Reynolds, and Arnold (2006).

8. Jones, Reynolds, and Arnold (2006).

9. Kang (2009).

10. Gabriel and Lang (1995), p. 107.

11. Saunders (2005), p. 48.

12. Gladwell (1996).

13. O'Donnell (2008).

References

Anonymous. (2002a). 1962 to 1972: The birth of discounting. *DSN Retailing Today, 41*(15), 7–11.

Anonymous. (2002b). 1972 to 1982: Discounters grow up and catalog showrooms emerge. *DSN Retailing Today, 41*(15), 13–19.

Anonymous. (2002c). 1982 to 1992: Clubs and category killers arrive on the scene. *DSN Retailing Today, 41*(15), 21–25.

Anonymous. (2010d). Top Ten Trends in Retail. What Next: *http://www.nowandnext.com* accessed 28 August 2010.

Arnold, M., & Reynolds, K. (2003). Hedonic shopping motivations. *Journal of Retailing, 79*(2), 77–95.

Babin, B., Darden, W., & Griffin, M. (1994). Work and/or fun: Measuring hedonic and utilitarian shopping values. *Journal of Consumer Research, 20*(4), 644–656.

Baker, J., Levy, M., & Grewal, D. (1992). An experimental approach to making retail store environmental decisions. *Journal of Retailing, 68*(4), 445.

Baker, J., Parasuraman, A., Grewal, D., & Voss, G. B. (2002). The influence of multiple store environment cues on perceived merchandise value and patronage intentions. *Journal of Marketing, 66*(2), 120–141.

Bamossy, G. (1982). Socializing experiences as predictors of performing arts patronage behavior. *Journal of Cultural Economics, 6*(2), 37–44.

Barletta, M. (2003). *Marketing to women: How to understand, reach, and increase your share of the world's largest market segment.* Chicago, IL: Dearborn Trade Publishing.

Baron, S., Harris, K., & Harris, R. (2001). Retail theater: The "intended effect" of the performance. *Journal of Service Research, 4*(2), 102–117.

Beatty, S., Mayer, M., Coleman, J., Reynolds, K., & Lee, J. (1996). Customer-sales associate retail relationships. *Journal of Marketing, 72*(3), 223–247.

Belch, G., Belch, M. A., & Ceresino, G. (1985). Parental and teenage influences in family decision-making. *Journal of Business Research, 13*(2), 163–176.

Benson, S. P. (1986). *Counter cultures: Saleswomen, managers, and customers in American department stores, 1880–1940.* Champaign, IL: University of Illinois Press.

Bloch, P. H., Ridgway, N. M., & Dawson, S. A. (1994). The shopping mall as consumer habitat. *Journal of Retailing, 70*(1), 23-43.

Borges, A., Chebat, J. C., & Babin, B. J. (2010). Does a companion always enhance the shopping experience? *Journal of Retailing and Consumer Services, 17*(4), 294–299.

Boosler, Elayne. (2010). Accessed August 23, 2010, from http://www.notable andquotable.com

Bristor, J., & Fischer, E. (1993). Feminist thought: Implications for consumer research. *Journal of Consumer Research, 19*(4)518–536.

Brown, D. (2002, July 15). Is retail ready to buy training? *Canadian HR Reporter, 15*(13), 7.

Burns, D., & Rayman, D. (1995). Retailing in Canada and the United States: Historical comparisons. *Service Industries Journal, 15*(4), 164–176.

Cameron, D. (2003, June 21). Money, work, and family send stress levels soaring. *The Age,* News, 5.

Campbell, C. (1997). Shopping, pleasure, and the sex war. In P. Falk & C. Campbell (Eds.), *The Shopping Experience.* London, England: Sage, 166–76.

Cardoso, P. R., & Pinto, S. C. (2010). Hedonic and utilitarian shopping motivations among Portuguese young adult consumers. *International Journal of Retail & Distribution Management, 38*(7), 538–558.

Chiaro, A. (Executive Producer). (2010, August 6). *Weekend Today Show* [Television broadcast]. New York, NY: NBC News.

Chung, C. J. (2001). Ms. Consumer. In C. J. Chung, J. Inaba, R. Koolhas, & S. T. Leong (Eds.), *Harvard Design School Guide to Shopping.* New York, NY: Taschen, 505–25.

Church, L. M., & Thomas, A. R. (2006). *Shoppers' Paradise Lost: Shopping by elderly adults in the age of big-box businesses.* Working Paper: Center for Social Science Research. State University of New York, Oneonta. http://www .oneonta.edu/academics/ssr/PDF/Elderly%20Shopping.pdf

Cole-Gomolski, B. (1998, June 15). Training benefits scrutinized, link to profitability hard to prove. *Computerworld, 32*(24), 24.

Costa, J. A. (1994). *Gender issues and consumer behavior.* Thousand Oaks, CA: Sage.

Cox, A., Cox, D. C., & Anderson, R. (2005). Reassessing the pleasures of store shopping. *Journal of Business Research, 58*(3), 250–259.

Csikszentmihalyi, M. (1997). *Finding flow: The psychology of engagement with everyday life.* New York, NY: Harper Perennial.

Darian, J. C. (1998). Parent-child decision-making in children's clothing stores. *International Journal of Retail & Distribution Management, 26*(11), 421–428.

d'Astous, A. (2000). Irritating aspects of the shopping environment. *Journal of Business Research, 49*(2), 149–156.

Dholakia, R. R. (1999). Going shopping: Key determinants of shopping behaviors and motivations. *International Journal of Retail & Distribution Management, 27*(4), 154–165.

Dotson, M., & Patton, W. E., III. (1992). Consumer perceptions of department store service: A lesson for retailers. *Journal of Services Marketing, 6*(2), 15–28.

Douglas, S. (1994). *Where the girls are: Growing up female with the mass media.* New York, NY: Times Books.

Eroglu, S., & Harrell, G. (1986). Retail crowding: Theoretical and strategic implications. *Journal of Retailing, 62*(4), 346–363.

Eroglu, S. A., & Machleit, K. A. (1990). An empirical study of retail crowding: Antecedents and consequences. *Journal of Retailing, 66*(2), 201–221.

Falk, P., & Campbell, C. (1997). *The shopping experience.* London, England: Sage.

Feick, L. F., & Price, L. L. (1987). The market maven: A diffuser of marketplace information. *Journal of Marketing, 51*(1), 83–97.

Feinberg, R., & Meoli, J. (1991). A brief history of the mall. *Advances in Consumer Research, 18*(1), 426–427.

Feinberg, R., Sheffler, B., Meoli, J. & Rummel, A. (1989). There's something social happening at the mall. *Journal of Business and Psychology*, 4(1), 49-63.

Fischer, E., & Arnold, S. J. (1990). More than a labor of love: Gender roles and Christmas gift shopping. *Journal of Consumer Research, 17*(3), 333.

Fischer, E., Gainer, B., & Bristor, J. (1997). The sex of the service provider: Does it influence perceptions of service quality? *Journal of Retailing, 73*(3), 361–382.

Fischer, E., Gainer, B., & Bristor, J. (1998). Beauty Salon and Barber Shop: gendered servicescapes. In J. Sherry (Ed.), *Servicescapes: The concept of place in contemporary markets.* pp. 565-590. Lincolnwood, IL: NTC Business Books.

Fisher, R. J., & Dubé, L. (2005). Gender differences in responses to emotional advertising: A social desirability perspective. *Journal of Consumer Research, 31*(4), 850–858.

Francis, S., Burns, L. (1992), Effect of consumer socialization on clothing shopping attitudes, clothing acquisition, and clothing satisfaction, *Clothing and Textiles Research Journal, 10*(4), 35–39.

Franke, G. R., & Park, J.-E. (2006). Salesperson adaptive selling behavior and customer orientation: A meta-analysis. *Journal of Marketing Research, 43*(4), 693–702.

Gabriel, Y., & Lang, T. (1995). *The unmanageable consumer.* London, England: Sage.

Gavish, Y., Shoham, A., & Ruvio, A. (2008). A qualitative study of mother–adolescent daughter vicarious role model consumption interactions. *Advances in Consumer Research: North American Conference Proceedings, 35*, 732–734.

Gladwell, M. (1996, November 4). The science of shopping. *The New Yorker,* 66+.

Glass, J., Bengston, V. L., & Dunham, C. C. (1986). Attitude similarity in three-generation families: Socialization, status inheritance, or reciprocal influence. *American Sociological Review, 51*(5), 685–698.

Goff, B. G., Bellenger, D. N, & Stojack, C. (1994). Cues to consumer susceptibility to salesperson influence: Implications for adaptive retail selling. *Journal of Personal Selling & Sales Management, 14*(2), 25.

Gorz, A. (1989). *Critique of economic reason.* London, UK: Verso. Cited in Worpole, K. (1992). *Towns for people: Transforming urban life.* Buckingham: Open University Press.

Graham, D. F., Graham, I., & MacLean, M. J. (1991). Going to the mall: A leisure activity of urban elderly people. *Canadian Journal on Aging, 10*(4), 345–358.

Green, E. (1998). Women doing friendship: An analysis of women's leisure as a site of identity construction, empowerment, and resistance. *Leisure Studies, 17,(3),* 171–185.

Harrison, M. (1975). *People and shopping.* London, England: Ernest Benn.

Haytko, D. L., & Baker, J. (2004). It's all at the mall: Exploring adolescent girls' experiences. *Journal of Retailing, 80*(1), 67–83.

Healy, M., Beverland, M., Oppewal, H., & Sands, S. (2007). Understanding retail experiences: The case for ethnography. *International Journal of Market Research, 49*(6), 751–778.

Hine, T. (2002). *I want that: How we all became shoppers.* New York, NY: HarperCollins.

Hirschman, E., & Holbrook, M. (1982). Hedonic consumption: Emerging concepts, methods, and propositions. *Journal of Marketing, 46 (3),* 92–101.

Hoover Company Records. (2006a). Amway history. Retrieved October 30, 2006, from Proquest database.

Hoover Company Records. (2006b). Avon History. Retrieved October 30, 2006, from Proquest database.

Hoover Company Records. (2006c). eBay History. Retrieved October 30, 2006, from Proquest database.

Hu, H., & Jasper, C. Y. (2006). Social cues in the store environment and their impact on store image. *International Journal of Retail & Distribution Management, 34*(1), 25–48.

Huddleston, P. T., Whipple, J., & Cho, D. (2010). *Effects of hedonic and utilitarian motivated values on shopping outcomes: Comparing conventional and specialty grocery stores.* Working Paper: Michigan State University.

Jones, M. A., Reynolds, K. E., & Arnold, M. J. (2006). Hedonic and utilitarian shopping value: Investigating differential effects on retail outcomes. *Journal of Business Research, 59*(9), 974.

Kacen, J. J. (1998). Retail therapy: Consumers' shopping cures for negative moods. *Advances in Consumer Research, 25*(1), 80.

Kacen, J. J., & Friese, S. (1999). An exploration of mood-regulating consumer buying behavior. *European Advances in Consumer Research, 4*(1), 75–76.

Kang, M. (2009). *Retail therapy: A qualitative investigation and scale development* (Doctoral dissertation, University of Minnesota). Retrieved from Dissertations & Theses @ CIC Institutions (Publication No. AAT 3358664).

Kershaw, P. (2003, March 22). We need to talk: Building a relationship with women. *Sydney Morning Herald,* Business, 85.

Kiecker, P., & Hartman, C. L. (1993). Purchase pal use: Why buyers choose to shop with others. *Proceedings of the AMA Winter Educators' Conference.* Varadarajan, R. & Bernard Jaworski, B. eds. (pp. 378–384). Chicago, IL: American Marketing Association.

Kim, Y. K., Kim, E. Y., & Kang, J. (2003). Teens' mall shopping motivations: Functions of loneliness and media usage. *Family and Consumer Sciences Research Journal, 32* (2), 140–167.

Kim Y. K., Sullivan, P., & Forney, J. C. (2007). *Experiential retailing: Concepts and strategies that sell.* New York, NY: Fairchild Publications.

Kleinberg, S. J. (1999). *Women in the United States, 1830–1945.* New Brunswick, NJ: Rutgers University Press.

Kotler, P. (1973/74). Atmospherics as a marketing tool. *Journal of Retailing, 49*(4), 48–65.

Kozinets, R. V., Sherry, J. F., DeBerry-Spence, B., Duhachek, A., Nuttavuthisit, K., & Storm, D. (2002). Themed flagship brand stores in the new millennium: Theory, practice, prospects. *Journal of Retailing, 78*(1), 17–29.

Lachance, M. J., & Choquette-Bernie, N. (2004). College students' consumer competence: A qualitative exploration. *International Journal of Consumer Studies, 28*(5), 433–442.

Lai, M. K., & Aritejo, B. A. (2009). To bargain or not to bargain? Determinants of consumer intention to bargain in the retail market. *Advances in Consumer Research: Asia-Pacific Conference Proceedings,* 8, 160–161.

Lambert, C. (2003, April 13). They're young, single, and spending $11 billion. *Sunday Mail,* News, 3.

Landry, T. D., Arnold, T. J., & Arndt, A. (2005). A compendium of sales-related literature in customer relationship management: Processes and technologies with managerial implications. *Journal of Personal Selling & Sales Management, 25*(3), 231–251.

Leonards, S. (2010). Retrieved April 23, 2010, from http://www.stewleonards.com

Lowndes, S. F., & Moore, R. L. (1975). Price accuracy as a consumer skill. *Journal of Advertising Research, 15*(4), 27–34.

Luo, X. (2005). How does shopping with others influence impulsive purchasing? *Journal of Consumer Psychology, 15*(4), 288–294.

Maloney, G. (2002). Gen Y and the future of mall retailing. Jones Lang LaSalle. Retrieved August 29, 2010, from http://www.us.am.joneslanglasalle.com/Lists/ExpertiseInAction/Attachments/255/JLL-Gen-Y-Mall-Retailing.pdf

Maloney, G. (2005).When cohorts collide. Jones Lang LaSalle. Retrieved August 29, 2010, from http://www.us.am.joneslanglasalle.com/Lists/ExpertiseInAction/Attachments/253/JLL-Cohorts-Collide.pdf

Martin, C. A. (2009). Consumption motivation and perceptions of malls: A comparison of mothers and daughters. *Journal of Marketing Theory and Practice, 17*(1), 49–61.

May, E. T. (2000). Pushing the limits, 1940–1961. In N. F. Cott (Ed.), *No small courage* (pp. 472–528). New York, NY: Oxford University Press.

McGrath, M. A. (1998). Dream on: Projections of an ideal servicescape. In J. F. Sherry (Ed.), *Servicespaces: The concept of place in contemporary markets*. Chicago, IL: NTC Business Books, 439–53.

McGregor, J. (2008, October 9). Costco's artful discounts. *Business Week*. Retrieved June 21, 2010, from http://www.hhcpublishing.com/news/2008_1009_businessweek.pdf

Meltzer, M. (2010, March 22). The thrill of the haul: The secret joy of displaying your shopping sprees on YouTube. *Slate.com*. Retrieved June 15, 2010, from http://www.slate.com/toolbar.aspx?action=print&id=2248295

Mettler, S. (2005). *Soldiers to citizens: The GI Bill and the making of the greatest generation*. New York, NY: Oxford University Press.

Meyer, D. J. C., & Anderson, H. C. (2000). Preadolescents and apparel purchasing: Conformity to parents and peers in the consumer socialization process. *Journal of Social Behavior and Personality, 15*(2), 243–257.

Meyers-Levy, J. (1989). Priming effects on product judgments: A hemispheric interpretation. *Journal of Consumer Research, 16*(1), 76–86.

Meyers-Levy, J., & Sternthal, B. (1991). Gender differences in the use of message cues and judgments. *Journal of Marketing Research, 28*(1), 84–96.

Miller, R.K. (2009). Generational focus. In *Media and advertising market research handbook* (pp. 157–166). Loganville, GA: Richard K. Miller & Associates.

Minahan, S. M., & Beverland, M. (2005). *Why women shop: Secrets revealed*. Melbourne, Australia: Wiley.

Mitchell, N., Oppewal, H., & Beverland, M. *ANZMAC 2009: Sustainable management and marketing conference*. Monash University, Melbourne, Australia.

Moore, E. S., Wilkie, W., & Alder, J. A. (2001). Lighting the torch: How do intergenerational influences develop? *Advances in Consumer Research, 28*(1), 287–293.

Moutinho, L., Davies, F., & Curry, B. (1996). The impact of gender on car buyer satisfaction and loyalty: A neural network analysis. *Journal of Retailing and Consumer Services, 3*(3), 135–144.

Muhlebach, R. (2003). A shopping odyssey. *Journal of Property Management, 68*(1), 34.

Myers-Levy, J. (1989). Priming effects on product judgments: A hemispheric interpretation. *Journal of Consumer Research, 16*(1), 76–85.

Nagle, B. (2002, July 15). Superior retail training blends customer service, product knowledge. *Canadian HR Reporter, 15*(13), 7–8.

Neeley, S. (2005). Influences on consumer socialization. *Young Consumers, 6*(2), 63–69.

Neeley, S. M., & Coffey, T. (2007). Understanding the "four-eyed, four-legged" consumer: A segmentation analysis of U.S. moms. *Journal of Marketing Theory and Practice, 15*(3), 251–261.

Nelms, C. (n.d.). Retrieved August 23, 2010, from http://www.brainyquote.com/quotes/quotes/c/cynthianel137709.html

Nystrom, P. (1930). *Economics of retailing* (3rd ed., Vols. 1–2). New York, NY: Ronald Press.

O'Donnell, J. (2008, February 1). Some retailers tighten return policies. *USA Today*, 3B.

Oldenburg, R. (2000). *Celebrating the Third Place: Inspiring stories about the "great good places" at the heart of our communities.* New York, NY: Marlowe & Company.

Otnes, C., & McGrath, M. A. (2001). Perceptions and realities in male shopping behavior. *Journal of Retailing 77(1)*, 111–137.

Peters, T. in Barletta, M. (2003). *Marketing to women: How to understand, reach, and increase your share of the world's largest market segment.* Chicago, IL: Dearborn Trade Publishing.

Pettigrew, S. (2007). Reducing the experience of loneliness among older consumers. *Journal of Research for Consumers 12*, 1–4.

Pettijohn, L. S., & Pettijohn, C. E. (1994). Retail sales training. *Journal of Services Marketing, 8*(3), 17–26.

Pine, B. J., & Gilmore, J. H. (1999). *The experience economy: Work is theater and every business a stage.* Boston, MA: Harvard Business Press.

Popcorn, F., and Marigold, L. (2000). *EVEolution: The eight truths of marketing to women.* New York, NY: Hyperion Books.

Protyniak, N. (2003, July 9). The great sex divide. *Herald Sun*, Durham, NC, 8.

Puente, M. (2006, April 17). "Aisles and aisles of good times: Life trends in Supermarkets." *USA Today*, p. 01D.

Rappaport, E. D. (2000). *Shopping for pleasure: Women in the making of London's West End.* Princeton, NJ: Princeton University Press.

Razer, H. (2007, December 26). It's where we go to be together with our loved ones: Chaddy. *The Age*, Section 1, 15.

Rhode, C. (2006). Making the right decision. *Chain Store Age Executive, 82*(3), 127.

Rowe, P. (2003). *Secret women's business: How to get it all and keep it.* Sydney, Australia: New Holland Publishers.

Rust, L. (1993). Observations: Parents and children shopping together: A new approach to the qualitative analysis of observational data. *Journal of Advertising Research, 33*(4), 65–70.

Sandikci, O., & Holt, D. B. (1998). Malling society: Mall consumption practices and the future of public space. In J. Sherry (Ed.), *Servicescapes: The concept of place in contemporary markets* (pp. 305–336). Lincolnwood, IL: NTC Business Books.

SanFilippo, M. (2005). Family Dollar experiences challenging quarter. *Home Textiles Today, 26*(41), 6.

Saunders, W. S. (2005). *Commodification and Spectacle in Architecture: a Harvard Design Magazine Reader.* Minneapolis, MN: University of Minnesota Press.

Savitt, R. (1989). Looking back to see ahead: Writing the history of American retailing. *Journal of Retailing, 65*(3), 326–355.

Schindler, R. M. (1989). The excitement of getting a bargain: Some hypotheses concerning the origin and effects of smart-shopper feelings. In T. K. Srull (Ed.), *Advances in consumer research* (pp. 447–453). Provo, UT: Association for Consumer Research.

Schindler, R., Lala, V., & Grussenmeyer-Corcoran, C. (2008). Intergenerational influence in consumer deal proneness. *Advances in Consumer Research: North American Conference Proceedings, 35,* 735–736.

Schmitt, B. (1999). *Experimental marketing,* New York, NY: Free Press.

Schroeder, J. (2003). Introduction to special issue: Consumption, gender, and identity. *Consumption, Markets, and Culture, 6*(1), 1–4.

Shao, C. Y., Baker, J. A., & Wagner, J. (2004). The effects of appropriateness of service contact personnel dress on customer expectations of service quality and purchase intention: The moderating influences of involvement and gender. *Journal of Business Research, 57*(10), 1164–1176.

Sharma, A., & Stafford, T. F. (2000). The effect of retail atmospherics on customers' perceptions of salespeople and customer persuasion: An empirical investigation. *Journal of Business Research, 49*(2), 183–191.

Sherman, E., Schiffman, L. G., & Mathur, A. (2001). The influence of gender on the new-age elderly's consumption orientation. *Psychology & Marketing, 18*(10), 1073–1089.

Shop. (2003). In *Merriam-Webster's online dictionary* (11th ed.). Retrieved from http://www.merriam-webster.com/dictionary/shop

Silverstein, M. J. (2006). *Treasure hunt: Inside the mind of the new consumer.* New York, NY: Portfolio.

Smith, M. D. (2008) *Women's roles in seventeenth-century America*. Westport, CT: Greenwood Press.

Sorce, P., Loomis, L., & Tyler, P. R. (1989). Intergenerational influence on consumer decision making. *Advances in Consumer Research, 16*(1), 271–275.

Tauber, E. M. (1995). Why do people shop? *Marketing Management, 4*(2), 58.

Thompson, C. (1996). Caring consumers: Gendered consumption meanings and the juggling lifestyle. *Journal of Consumer Research 22*(4), 399.

Tingley, J., & Robert, L. (2000). *Gendersell: How to sell to the opposite sex*. New York, NY: Touchstone Books.

Underhill, P. (2000). *Why we buy: The science of shopping*. New York, NY: Simon & Schuster.

U.S. Census Bureau. (2007). Current population survey 2007. Retrieved from http://www.census.gov/population/www/socdemo/educ-attn.html. Accessed February 15, 2010.

U.S. Census Bureau. (2008a). The 2008 statistical abstract. Shopping centers: Gross leasable area and sales by state. Retrieved from http://www.census.gov/compendia/statab/2008/tables/08s1031.pdf. Accessed October 27, 2010

U.S. Census Bureau. (2008b). Employed civilians by occupation, sex, race and Hispanic origin: 2008. Retrieved from http://www.census.gov/compendia/statab/2010/tables/10s0603.pdf Accessed February 15, 2010.

U.S. National Center for Health Statistics. (2009). Deaths: Final Data for 2006. *National Vital Statistics Reports (NVSR), 57*(14). Atlanta, GA: Center for Disease Control and Prevention.

Viswanathan, M., Childers, T. L., & Moore, E. S. (2000). The measurement of intergenerational communication and influence on consumption: Development, validation, and cross-cultural comparison of the IGEN scale. *Journal of the Academy of Marketing Science, 28,* 406–424.

Voigt, K. (2009, October 25). Women: Saviors of the world economy. *CNN.com*. Retrieved February 15, 2010 from http://edition.cnn.com/2009/WORLD/asiapcf/10/25/intl.women.global.economy/index.html?iref=storysearch.

Walsh, G., Gwinner, K. P., & Swanson, S. R. (2004). What makes mavens tick? Exploring the motives of market mavens' initiation of information diffusion. *Journal of Consumer Marketing*, 21(2/3), 109-122.

Ward, J. C., Bitner, M. J., & Barnes, J. (1992). Measuring the prototypicality and meaning of retail environments. *Journal of Retailing, 68*(2), 194–220.

Ward, S. (1974). Consumer socialization. *Journal of Consumer Research*, 1(2), 1-14.

Ward, S., Wackman, D. B., & Wartella, E. (1977). *How children learn to buy: The development of consumer information processing skills*. Beverly Hills, CA: Sage.

Weitz, B. A., Bradford, K. D. (1999). Personal selling and sales management: A relationship marketing perspective. *Journal of the Academy of Marketing Science, 27*(2), 241–254.

Woodruffe, H. R. (1997). Compensatory consumption: Why women go shopping when they're fed up and other stories. *Marketing Intelligence & Planning, 15*(7), 325–334.

Woodruffe-Burton, H. (1998). Private desires, public display: Consumption, postmodernism, and fashion's "new man." *International Journal of Retail & Distribution Management, 26*(8), 301.

Yurchisin, J., Ruoh-Nan, Y., Watchravesringkan, K., & Chen, C. (2006). Why retail therapy? A preliminary investigation of the role of liminality, self-esteem, negative emotions, and the proximity of clothing to self in the compensatory consumption of apparel products. *Advances in Consumer Research: Asia-Pacific Conference Proceedings 5,* 730–731.

Zola, É. (1883/1995). The Ladies' Paradise (Au bonheur des dames). B. Nelson (Trans.). Oxford, England: Oxford University Press.

Index

Announcing the Business Expert Press Digital Library

Concise E-books Business Students Need for Classroom and Research

This book can also be purchased in an e-book collection by your library as

- a one-time purchase,
- that is owned forever,
- allows for simultaneous readers,
- has no restrictions on printing, and
- can be downloaded as PDFs from within the library community.

Our digital library collections are a great solution to beat the rising cost of textbooks. e-books can be loaded into their course management systems or onto student's e-book readers.

The BUSINESS EXPERT PRESS digital libraries are very affordable, with no obligation to buy in future years.

For more information, please visit WWW.BUSINESSEXPERT.COM/LIBRARIES. To set up a trial in the United States, please contact SHERI ALLEN at *sheri.allen@globalepress.com*; for all other regions, contact NICOLE LEE at **NICOLE.LEE@IGROUPNET.COM**.

OTHER TITLES IN OUR CONSUMER BEHAVIOR COLLECTION

Series Editor: Naresh Malhotra

Store Design by Claus Ebster

3 9547 00358 7875

658.834
HUD

Huddleston, Patricia.
Consumer behavior

FREE PUBLIC LIBRARY, SUMMIT, N.J.

JUL 2011